Meir Y. Soloveichik

SACRED TIME

The Tikvah Fund
Maggid Books

Sacred Time
First Edition, 2024

Maggid Books
An imprint of Koren Publishers Jerusalem Ltd.

POB 8531, New Milford, CT 06776-8531, USA
& POB 4044, Jerusalem 9104001, Israel
www.korenpub.com

Cover image: *The Conclusion of Sabbath* (Sabbath-Ausgang), 1866,
Moritz Daniel Oppenheim, Google Art Project, attribution: DcoetzeeBot

The publication of this book was made possible
through the generous support of *The Jewish Book Trust*.

ISBN 978-1-59264-632-6, *hardcover*

A CIP catalogue record for this title is
available from the British Library

Printed and bound in Turkey

For

Nicole and Raanan Agus
Cherished friends

&

Neal Kozodoy
Wise editor

With profound gratitude to
the leaders, partners, supporters, and staff of:

The Tikvah Fund

Koren Publishers Jerusalem

Yeshiva University's Straus Center
for Torah and Western Thought

Congregation Shearith Israel

The Paul E. Singer Foundation

For their generous support of this volume,
Tikvah extends its warmest thanks to

Nicole and Raanan Agus

of New York City and Jerusalem,

students and followers of Rabbi Meir Soloveichik
for the past two decades.

Contents

Introduction

The Secret of Jewish Endurance

I open with a sweeping statement: the Jewish calendar is a key that unlocks the very essence of Judaism.

How so? What is it about the calendar that justifies so blunt an assertion? What do I mean by my use of the phrase "*sacred* time," and what is so special about it?

Addressing such questions, some writers have suggested that Judaism in its entirety is a religion of sacred time, as distinct from other faiths that have elevated the concept of sacred *space*. Thus, pagans who worship finite gods see those deities as living in defined spatial enclosures; by contrast, the infinite and eternal Almighty is encountered within and through the boundless fluidity of time, whether historical or calendrical.

But this is not quite right. After all, Judaism does proclaim the inherent sanctity of, for instance, the finite land of Israel. And the Jewish romance with the city of Jerusalem, along with the millennia-long Jewish yearning for the restoration of its sanctity, fully rivals the age-old Jewish love affair with the Sabbath, the quintessential event in time.

A more balanced view is called for: The supreme Jewish insight is that holiness can inhere both in space *and* in time. To speak of a space as holy is to recognize that holiness as restricted to the site's boundaries. The land of Israel, in Judaism, possesses a holiness that the rest of the earth does not; the specific sanctity of Jerusalem is not shared with the rest of the land of Israel; the Temple Mount retains a special status apart from the rest of Jerusalem.

> "Our experience of God's saving power in our history also enables a faith in the future."

In sacred time, of which the Sabbath is the supreme example, not the place but the day is saturated with holiness, not the grains of sand but the hours. And that holiness-saturated day can unite Jews – so long as they are sensitive to it, welcome it, bless it, and celebrate it – across the vastness of space, be they in the Far East (when daylight arrives there) or in the far reaches of the West (when it arrives there).

This is sacred time as encountered in the weekly Sabbath: a time when, to quote my great-uncle, Rabbi Joseph B. Soloveitchik, "days and hours are saturated with holiness."[1] Also special about the Sabbath is that it is first and foremost a commemoration of *creation*: the recalling of a moment that occurred long before there were Jews. In the calendar, by contrast, sacred times memorialize covenantal moments in Jewish *history*.

And here an even more extraordinary idea introduces itself, one whose nuances and implications we shall unfold as we go along. For if, for Jews, the sanctity of Jewish time extends everywhere on earth, and overcomes all manner of physical separation, the same goes for all manner of temporal or historical separations. Through its calendar, Rabbi Soloveitchik suggests, "Judaism developed a very particular philosophy of memory – indeed, an ethics of memory. One does not simply recollect the past, or just remember bygones but *re-experiences* that which has been, and quickens events that are seemingly dead."

At the Passover Seder, which we shall encounter in chapter 7, we re-experience the Exodus from Egypt. In the synagogue on Shavuot (ch. 9), we recite the Ten Commandments and instinctively rise from our seats in the certainty that we, too, are standing like our ancestors at the foot of Mount Sinai and hearing for the first time the voice of the Almighty.

Verses in the Torah itself signal this age-old orientation. "Because of *this* did God act for me when I went forth from Egypt" (Ex. 13:8), the Torah says, thereby obligating us to convey these same words to our children, establishing for all time that not only our ancestors but we as well were redeemed from Egypt.

Next, and perhaps even more intriguingly: "You shall tell your children and grandchildren of the day that you stood before the Lord your God at Sinai" (Deut. 4:9–10). By teaching our offspring that each of us, in every generation, has stood at Sinai, the event becomes as real for them as it is for us – a reality that they, in turn, can re-enact for, and transmit to, their own children. Thanks to this generational link, notes Rabbi Soloveitchik, "bygones turn into facts, pale memories into living experiences, and archaeological history into a vibrant reality."[2]

And there is still more. "On this night" – as Jews cry out on the fast of the ninth of Av – we bemoan the destruction of the ancient Temple in Jerusalem as if it were still burning right in front of our eyes. More frequently, however, it is not tragedy but the prospect of divine *redemption* that insists on retaining its prominence in Jewish memory. We are not only the receptacles of an eternally living past; our experience of God's saving power in our history also enables a faith in the future. To some extent, this aspect of our faith even allows us to experience the future as if *it* has already happened.

Consider for a moment the astonishing words of the prophet Isaiah as he first describes Israel lamenting Jerusalem's destruction – "Zion said, 'God has forsaken me, and my Lord has forgotten me'" (49:14) – only to follow almost immediately afterward with words of consolation and, in a sudden grammatical shift, with a vision of ultimate redemption as if the promised consolation has already occurred: "For God has comforted Zion and all its waste places, has made its wilderness into Eden and its desert into the garden of the

Lord wherein joy and gladness can be found, thanksgiving and the voice of melody" (51:3). In our era, this last verse, read every year in the weeks following the great fast of the ninth of Av, has been at least partially fulfilled in the miracle of modern Israel.

It is this aspect of Jewish time that so sustained Jews throughout the centuries as they marked Passover, the Festival of Freedom, while restrained within the suffocating walls of a ghetto, celebrated Sinai while exiled across the earth, or observed the holiness of Yom Kippur, the "Day of Atonement," while locked by a dictator in a prison cell. If Jews could endure amidst persecution and pogroms, it was thanks to the extraordinary audaciousness of Isaiah's prophetic vision of the Temple rebuilt. If, when everything seemed hopeless, the Jewish people found the strength to survive, it was thanks to the phenomenal faith of a Rabbi Akiva who, even while mourning the Roman army's massacre of Jerusalem's Jews, stubbornly invoked the wondrous spectacle, in the uplifting words of the prophet Zechariah, of grandfathers and grandmothers once again gazing with delight at their grandchildren at play on the sidewalks of a Jerusalem restored, and sharing with their little ones the memory of the time they themselves merited to stand at Sinai.

In sum: To encounter the rhythms of the Jewish calendar, to comprehend its commemorations, is not merely to understand the significance of each joyous holiday and each moment of mourning, each feast and each fast. It is also to partake of the ability to unite East with West, to journey between past and present, and to set forth from the here-and-now toward the redemption that is yet to be. It is to understand nothing less than the secret of Jewish endurance.

Before proceeding to this book's chapters, let's linger for a moment longer on the distinction between Sabbath and holidays that I identified briefly above. To help illustrate the Sabbath – a universal message, bequeathed to the world by the Jewish people – I offer a story of our time.

In February 2003, Ilan Ramon became the first Israeli astronaut to take part in the American space program by joining the crew of the space shuttle *Columbia*. While training for the flight at Cape Canaveral in Florida, Ramon – a hero of the Israeli Air Force and, in 1981, the youngest participant in a famous raid that incapacitated the

▲ Ilan Ramon

Iraqi nuclear reactor at Osirak – turned to a local rabbi with a highly original question in the area of Jewish religious law. Seeing himself on this forthcoming flight as a representative not only of his country but of the Jewish people everywhere, he intended to mark, while in space, the onset of the Sabbath – and to do so while holding a goblet that he was taking along with him, filling it with wine, and pronouncing the special prayer that sanctifies the arrival of the Sabbath.

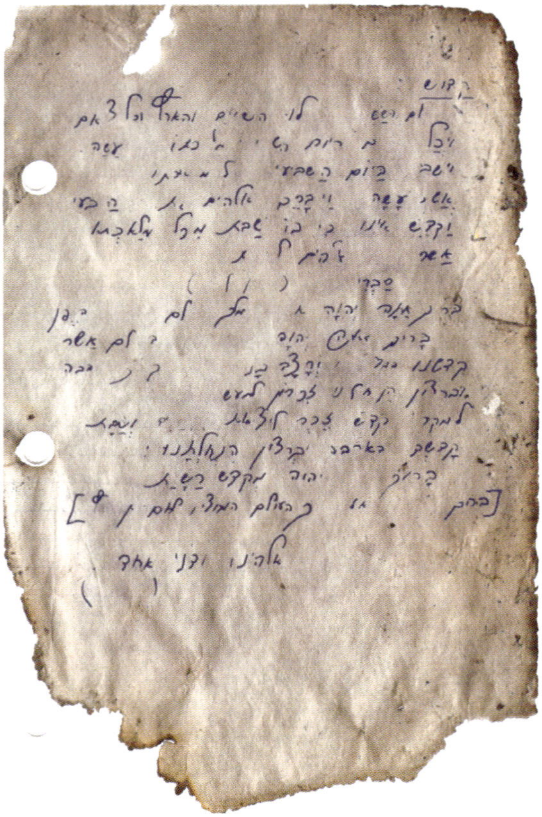

▲
Kiddush, from the remains of Ilan Ramon's diary

His problem, as the rabbi described it: How *does* one mark the advent of a particular moment in time in a situation where one is passing constantly through past and future, where a sunset occurs every ninety minutes, a new "week" every ten and a half hours, and a "new year" every twenty days?

Ramon's dilemma was circulated by the rabbi to scholars throughout the world, inspiring a lively discussion. In the end, he was advised to mark the onset of the Sabbath according to the time in Cape Canaveral. And thus, to this day, we have a stunning image of a Jew, floating in the heavens and sailing among the stars, as he is vocally commemorating God's creation of the universe in six days and blessing the Sabbath, the day of God's rest, over a cup of wine.

Tragically, this was one of the last moments of Ilan Ramon's life. Upon attempting reentry to the earth, the *Columbia* disintegrated, and he and all of the American astronauts aboard were lost to their loved ones and fellow citizens.

But they were not entirely lost. Several months later, remains of the *Columbia* were discovered in a field in Texas, and amidst the wreckage was Ramon's diary. Having survived the explosion, the fall through the atmosphere, and months of rain, the notebook was nevertheless in a condition to be reconstructed and studied. Among the words on the pages was the text of the Kiddush, the millennia-old prayer of sanctification, handwritten by Ramon in preparation for his journey.

At a NASA memorial service, the rabbi to whom Ramon had addressed his question mused on the circumstance that the legacy of this military hero would now be bound up forever with his unusual attention to Jewish religious law. Ramon, he reflected, taught us in his sanctification of a Shabbat that "no matter how fast we're going,we need to stop and ponder why God has put us here on earth."

And that, ultimately, is the message of Shabbat. Why, asked the eighteenth-century sage known as the Gaon of Vilna (1720–1797), *did* God put a stop to creation after six days? The answer: to show us that what we create becomes meaningful only once we stop creating it and start remembering why it was worth creating in the first place. This is the Sabbath: an idea, universal in nature, whose point, as the writer Judith Shulevitz once put it, is that in our lives we must remember to stop because we must stop in order to remember.

By their mindfulness in keeping and observing the Sabbath down through the generations, the Jews have faithfully proclaimed that message to all humanity.

What, then, about the holidays? They, by contrast, along with the annual calendar on which they are based, are not universal but, as I noted earlier, covenantal. They mark moments in Jewish history and embody the message of what might best be thought of as Jewish *particularity*.

For Jewish tradition, therefore, the calendar, which every year indicates when the observance of each holiday begins and when it ends, is an irreplaceable resource. And that calendar is itself linked to an astronomical phenomenon that for centuries has symbolized the particular uniqueness of the Jewish experience.

What is that phenomenon? It is the moon, on whose monthly cycle the Hebrew calendar (like that of a handful of others in the world) is based. How does this work? In summary: Because each month in the moon's regular cycle of phases is between twenty-nine and thirty days in length, Hebrew months tend also to alternate between twenty-nine and thirty days. And because those months are lunar, each of them begins at the sighting of the earliest visible crescent – the birth of the "new" moon – whose light waxes gradually toward full illumination at roughly mid-month and then wanes toward darkness over the next two weeks (or so) before the cycle starts all over again.

But there's also more to the story than that. For Jews, the lunar cycle has always been linked to the Exodus from Egypt, which occurred at full moon in the Hebrew month of Nisan, the month specifically named by God as "the first of the months of the year" (Ex. 12:2). And the moon is linked not just to the Exodus. According to tradition, the very first commandment given to the Israelites on the eve of that event – "You shall observe the [Feast of] Unleavened Bread, for on this very day I brought your ranks out of the land of Egypt; you shall observe this day throughout the ages as an institution for all time" (12:17) – would obligate the linkage of *all* Jewish holidays to the waxing and waning of the moon. Thus, if the advent of Passover in the spring and Sukkot in the fall occurs in mid-month to coincide with a *full* moon, Rosh HaShanah, which takes place on the first of the month (*Rosh Ḥodesh*) of Tishrei, always coincides with the *new* moon.

Why did the Jewish calendar become linked to the lunar cycle at the very moment of the Exodus? The reason, according to rabbinic tradition, is that the moon itself embodies the essence of the Jewish people. In its seeming disappearance into darkness, only to be suddenly reborn, the ancient rabbis saw the ultimate symbol of the eternal people: a nation born as it emerged from the night of slavery into the daylight of liberty. The Talmud – the great record of rabbinic discussion and teachings – informs us that during periods of persecution, when the observance of Jewish ritual was restricted, and circulating the year's calendar was forbidden, there existed a secret Hebrew code for announcing the arrival of a new moon: *David melekh Yisrael ḥai v'kayam* ("David, king of Israel, lives"). In other words: Judaism survives, the Jewish people endures.

All of this is embodied in the slender sliver of light reborn in the midst of darkness. As the Talmud insists, Jews see in the renewal of the moon's light a rendezvous between themselves and their Father in heaven, a reminder of God's promises to His people, the indelibility of the Torah and the eternity of the covenant, and the fact that, despite the insistence of others to the contrary, the never-superseded bond between Israel and God remains in place forever.

The Jewish observance of two sacred times – Shabbat on the one hand, and the holidays founded upon the lunar cycle on the other hand – represents the distinct nature of Jewish *existence*: at once a part of and apart from the world, at once chosen and linked to our connection with, and our monotheistic message to, humanity. Rabbi Samson Raphael Hirsch (1808–1888) put the dual point this way:

> From the onset of the creation, the Sabbath was an integral part of humankind, teaching men the awareness of their function as creatures and servants of God. [By contrast,] the new moon is a distinctive mark instituted at the start of Jewish history to serve as a catalyst for the understanding and fulfillment of the Jewish people's history. The Sabbath is the signature of our human existence, and the new moon the symbol of our particular Jewish calling.[3]

And what is that mixed calling? In the blessing recited over the Torah, we proclaim that we have been chosen from among the nations, but we never forget that part and parcel of our chosenness involves God's proclamation to Abraham: "Through you will all the families of the world be blessed" (Gen. 12:2). The renewal of the moon reminds Jews that we are chosen, but Judaism never lets us forget that we have been chosen as God's messenger to humanity.

Seen through the prism of modern cosmology, an interesting scientific parallel emerges here. The moon, as we know, orbits the earth, is bound to the earth, and might be seen by some as a rather insignificant astronomical addendum to the earth. Yet scientists, pondering what has been called the "Goldilocks paradox" – that is, why only in our world do the conditions seem to be "just right" for the emergence of sentient life? – have concluded that a large part of the answer has to do with what the French astronomer Jacques Laskar calls "our climate stability," a stability that owes its existence to "an exceptional event: the presence of the moon."[4] As the science journalist Fred Heeren describes the consensus view:

> Without an extra-large moon orbiting at the right distance from us,...earth would be subject to a runaway greenhouse effect as on Venus, or a permanent ice age such as Mars would experience if it had more water.[5]

Thus has the moon – minuscule as compared with other celestial bodies like the planets of our solar system – become positioned, against the odds, to play a crucial role in the survival of the human race. And thus has the Jewish people, a minuscule nation, vanishingly small when compared with other peoples and nations swirling in the solar system of societies and civilizations, been perfectly positioned, against the odds, to exercise a critical moral impact on humanity. "I will insist," said the great American founder John Adams,

> that the Hebrews have done more to civilize men than any other nation.... [Even] if I were an atheist...who believed that all is ordered by chance, I should believe that chance had ordered the Jews to...preserve and propagate to all mankind the doctrine of a supreme, intelligent, wise, almighty Sovereign of the universe, which I believe to be the great essential principle of all morality, and consequently all civilization.[6]

Says the Talmud: Israel calculates its years by keying its calendar to the moon while other nations – here it refers to Christian civilization – count by the sun (Sukkah 29a). This isn't a superficial statement of merely arbitrary calendrical preferences. Rather, the sages are implying, Israel has long been moonlike in its relation to other nations – revolving around those nations and never free to choose its own trajectory.

This might suggest that, logically, we Jews should have become extinct long ago. And yet not only have we survived but, separate from other people as the moon is separate from the earth while also indelibly affecting it, we have influenced and shaped the nature and destiny of the human race. Even in the darkest moments of its history, when it experienced nothing but hate from humanity, Israel understood that its mission was to be in connection *with* humanity. To cite Rabbi Samson Raphael Hirsch once again, "Jewish history is nothing but a moonlit reflection of how we have carried out our moral obligations – the moonlit resolution of our destiny."[7]

Ilan Ramon, the man who testified in orbit to the Jewish belief in the Creator of the universe, also, just before he died, testified to the eternal rebirth of the Jewish people. Along with his "Sabbath kit," he took with him into orbit a tiny Torah scroll that, decades earlier, in the Nazi concentration camp at Bergen-Belsen, belonged to a Dutch prisoner named Simon Dasberg, hitherto the esteemed chief rabbi of Amsterdam. Among its many other clandestine uses, the Torah had figured in the rabbi's preparation of another inmate, a young boy, Yoachim "Yoya" Joseph, for his bar mitzvah ceremony. The rabbi would perish in the camp; the boy to whom he had entrusted the precious Torah scroll would survive the Holocaust and later befriend and in turn entrust the scroll to Ilan Ramon.

In the *Columbia*, holding up Rabbi Dasberg's Torah, Ramon addressed his countrymen in Hebrew. "This," he said, "is a small Torah scroll that sixty years ago a child in Bergen-Belsen received from the rabbi of Amsterdam, who taught him from it in preparation for his bar mitzvah. And now it is with me in space." For one breathtaking moment, we can see Ramon, overcome with emotion, loosen his grip on the Torah, which begins to float further upward in the capsule toward the heavens.

Rabbi Dasberg's daughter, when interviewed in Israel following the space shuttle's disastrous end, suggested that the second life of the Torah scroll, whose remains would never be found, was both a sign of life from the past and a greeting dispatched to earth from heaven: an extraordinary emotional bond that more than anything represents the ability of the Jewish people to endure, to survive, and to thrive.

Shabbat, even as it unites Jews everywhere, marks God's creation of the whole world and His concern for all mankind; our Hebrew calendar, primarily lunar in essence, marks the covenantal uniqueness and chosenness of the people Israel. We proclaim both truths, and we will do so until both, as predicted by the prophets, are recognized by the world, and the verse in Isaiah is fulfilled: "It shall be on every new moon and Sabbath that all humanity will come to bow to Me, says the Lord" (66:23).

Let us begin.

CHAPTER ONE

Rosh HaShanah

▲ *The Anointing of Solomon, Cornelis de Vos*

No date in the Jewish calendar presents more diverse facets than the High Holy Day known as Rosh HaShanah. Instead of attempting to draw all of these facets together in a single chapter, my goal here is to highlight three central themes. Each of the three finds expression in the liturgy, each builds on one or more aspects of the other two, and each in its own way is made manifest in the shofar – the ancient musical instrument whose sound summons up for most Jews the mood and spirit of the entire High Holy Days season, and especially the ten days from Rosh HaShanah through Yom Kippur.

We can begin by noting that the most common statement made about Rosh HaShanah – namely, that it is the "Jewish New Year" – is, to be blunt, incorrect. True, the two Hebrew words do translate as "Head of the Year." In fact, however, the Jewish calendar marks at least two separate other years, and neither one of them is Rosh HaShanah as it has come to be known.

On Passover, during the spring month of Nisan, we commemorate every year the Exodus from Egypt and the birth of the Jewish people. The historical and calendrical significance of these events is stated explicitly, as we saw in the Introduction, in the book of Exodus: "This month [Nisan] shall be unto you the beginning of months" (12:2). In other words, this *is* the Jewish new year or, perhaps more exactly, the Jewish people's new year.

As for the second new year, it occurs three and a half months after Rosh HaShanah and one and a half months prior to Nisan. It is the festival of Tu BiShvat, the fifteenth day of the month of Shevat, known as *Rosh HaShanah LaIlanot,* the Jewish "new year for trees"; to it I devote chapter 5 in this book.

What, then, of Rosh HaShanah? On that two-day holiday, the inception of the ten-day period of introspection and repentance culminating in Yom Kippur, we commemorate nothing less than the creation not of the Jews but of the entire universe. Over and over again, the liturgy proclaims: *Hayom harat olam,* "Today is the birthday of the world" – and therefore the time, every year, when the *whole world* stands in judgment. This is the new year for humanity.

This introduces the first of our three themes, which is that in many ways, and in contrast to most other Jewish holidays, Rosh HaShanah is not particularistic in nature but universal. It is the day when, in commemorating God's creation of the world and all that is in it, we renew our fidelity to Him as King. Again and again, the Almighty is proclaimed *melekh al kol ha'aretz,* "king over *all* the earth." Again and again, we emphasize His universal monarchy and majesty, His absolute omniscience, omnipotence, and omnipresence, and our contrasting human frailty, fallibility, and mortality.

Indeed, it is to emphasize the kingship of God that the sound of the shofar is introduced in the Torah as a key element of Rosh HaShanah: the day "when the horn is sounded for you" (Num. 29:1).

The word "shofar," commonly rendered in English as a ram's horn, deserves its own explanation. In the Bible it refers simply to any kind of animal horn; only later did it become more narrowly defined as a ram's horn. These instruments were nothing less than the original coronation trumpets of the biblical age, a prominent feature in the ceremony marking the ascension of a flesh-and-blood Israelite king. For example: "And Zadok the priest took the vessel of oil out of the Tent, and anointed Solomon. And they blew the shofar; and all the people said: long live King Solomon!" (I Kings 1:39).

Indeed, that ancient Israelite ceremony would inspire and legitimize the monarchical procedures of at least one other worldly kingdom. For more than a thousand years, the crowning of an English king or queen has harked back to, and freely borrowed from, the very same language to be found in the biblical anointing of King Solomon. Here, from 1953, are the words of the archbishop of Canterbury in anointing Queen Elizabeth II: "As Solomon was anointed by Zadok the Priest and Nathan the prophet, so be thou anointed, blessed, and consecrated Queen over the peoples whom the Lord thy God hath given thee to govern."

> "Over and over again, the liturgy proclaims: *Hayom harat olam*, 'Today is the birthday of the world.'"

On Rosh HaShanah, then, the sound of the shofar is meant to evoke the majesty and authority of God as Creator and King, the providential overseer of the universe. The liturgy stresses in particular the great sounding of horns that accompanied the Almighty's entry into history and His revelation to the people of Israel at Mount Sinai, as "all the nation saw the thunder and the lightning, and the mountain afire, and the call of the shofar growing ever stronger" (Ex. 20:15).

In doing so, moreover, the liturgy looks at once back to the birth of the Jewish nation at Sinai and forward to the ultimate redemption of the world, reminding us not only of what was but also of what is yet to be when all whom God has created will recognize their absolute dependence on Him. "And it will be on that day, a great shofar will be sounded and all the lost… will come and worship the Lord on the holy mount, in Jerusalem" (Is. 27:13).

In the Ashkenazi tradition, the liturgical linking of the shofar and the majesty of God's kingship achieves its apotheosis in the section of the Rosh HaShanah service known by its first words as the *Untaneh tokef* ("Let us give voice to the power"). A great shofar is blown, all humanity is summoned before the divine judge, and, "as a shepherd herds his flock, directing his sheep to pass under his staff, so shall You cause to pass, count, and record the souls of all living, and decree the limit to each person's days, and inscribe their final judgment."

This is our first theme: God as the Creator and King of the universe, a theme resonating like a shofar blast everywhere in the prayer services on both days of Rosh HaShanah.

And yet, at the midway point in these services, something else occurs: Just as on every Sabbath and festival, the Torah scroll is taken out of the ark, escorted to the reader's desk, and placed at the center of the worshippers' attention. A part chosen specifically for each of the two days is then read, and is followed by its own specifically chosen *haftarah,* or reading from the prophets. It is in this critical interlude of the liturgy that our second theme emerges.

If you were designing the sacred Torah service on these most awesome of days, which scriptural readings would you choose? Which biblical texts would best reflect the resonant, fearsome, magisterial, and universal themes that are so exquisitely invoked and stressed in the liturgy?

Surely, one would think, and as Rabbi Jonathan Sacks noted, the Torah reading should itself commence with the earliest verses of Genesis: "In the beginning, God created the heavens and the earth…." Similarly with the reading from the prophets: perhaps a passage from Isaiah 45, for instance, with its declaration, "It is I who made the earth and created mankind upon it." Should not both of each day's scriptural texts parallel and complement the prayers? Should not their respective themes coincide with and reinforce each other?

Any one of these choices, as Rabbi Sacks put it, would make perfect, logical sense – but every one of them, he added, would be wrong. Instead, the readings from the Torah and the prophets contrast, almost blatantly, with the liturgy's focus on the creation of the world and God's kingship over all. Rather, they are about fathers and mothers, parents and children: about, in a word, family.

Thus, on the first day, the selection from the Torah concerns the miraculous advent of Isaac, the child born to a woman of ninety years and a man of one hundred. The parallel selection from the prophets is the story of Hannah, a childless woman who wants nothing more than the infant who, ultimately, will be given to her, whom she will name Samuel, and whom she will then consecrate to the service of God.

Before addressing these readings for the first day, let's dwell briefly on the family-centric theme itself – and, in this connection, let's note an additional fact about the shofar. Although the sounding of this horn was first understood as a manifestation of God's majesty and sovereignty over human history, in time it came to be interpreted as something else entirely: as a human cry, perhaps the cry of a mother, perhaps of a child, perhaps even of an infant at the moment of its birth. Today, in fact, researchers tell us that before newborns learn (at the age of about nine months) to adopt the specific linguistic intonations of their environments, it is impossible to differentiate their cries one from another; they all bawl alike. We might say that it is thus, too, on the birthday of the world, when the shofar, representing our helpless selves, marks not only the coronation of God but what might seem its exact opposite: the birth of a mewling, helpless infant.

So wherein lies the connection between the liturgy of majesty and these two readings from the Torah and the prophets – between the cosmic and the personal, the universal and the familial, between God as King and Creator, Judge and Redeemer, and us as decidedly lower-case parents and children? How can these two be reconciled?

The answer lies in Judaism's introduction of a startling, revolutionary notion of God's creation. If we cherish the relationship between parents and children, it is because *this* is the form of love that most imitates God's own love for humanity and God's particular love for His chosen people.

Rabbi Sacks cites a Jewish woman who joked, "Now that I'm a parent, I know what it's like to be God, because now I know what it's like to create someone you can't control." It's funny, but also true. If Rosh HaShanah is a remembrance of the time the universe was born, the most powerful way of reminding ourselves of the miracle of creation is to think about the only other similar miracle we know of. This – to have been bequeathed a creative capacity of our own – is what it means for us to have been created in the image of the Creator.

And in considering this, we also realize that our first two themes – the kingship of God and the parenthood of human beings – actually enhance one another. God is our King because He is our Creator, a fact that on Rosh HaShanah we seek to emphasize. Yet all the liturgical tropes in the world, all the verbal exclamations, all the metaphors at our disposal, cannot bring us to a comprehension of creation. No matter how vividly it is described, it cannot be imagined. But it can be intuitively grasped, and profoundly internalized and understood, when the cosmic is joined with the familial and when we, too, create a universe, however small, of our own.

Toward this end, the first chapter of Genesis about the creation of the world will do little to enlighten us, but the later chapters in Genesis, about our first fathers and mothers, are a big help. There is an old joke, told by the writer George Will, about the five-year-old child in a religious school who is busily drawing on a piece of paper. "What are you doing?" the teacher asks. The child replies: "I'm drawing a picture of God." The teacher objects: "Nobody knows what God looks like." The child replies: "They will, in five minutes." For in Hebrew Scripture, even if we cannot see God, we can see, in a mother and father's creation of a child, birthing of a child, and love for a child, what His love looks like.

Let me further illustrate this point with a personal anecdote from my own family. At the circumcision ceremony for our fifth child, my wife spoke about a conundrum pondered by medieval Jewish mystics: How is it that God, infinite and all-inclusive, could still make room for creation? Their answer to the puzzle invoked a process called in Hebrew *tzimtzum*, a kind of divine contraction, a sacrifice of God's own all-inclusiveness in order to allow a world to emerge into existence apart from and outside of His transcendent self.

Hannah and Samuel in the Temple, Rembrandt van Rijn or Rembrandt's studio

In explicating this notion, my wife invoked a parallel drawn in the twentieth century by Rabbi Joseph B. Soloveitchik: the parallel, that is, between the "sacrificial divine action" by which God made room for the universe, thereby creating a world to be cared for, sustained, and loved by Him, and the way in which a man and a woman, in becoming parents, "withdraw from their own self-centered romanticism into a love-oriented community"[1]: the family.

In "making room" for our own children, she said, our own lives as husband and wife had become more crowded but simultaneously more capacious, and our inner resources wondrously richer and more agile. She concluded: "I thank the Master of the Universe for the small but wonderful universe He has helped us fashion in our home."

Abraham and Isaac, Rembrandt van Rijn (1645)

And yet: lest we celebrate parenthood too unreservedly, we need to stop and apprehend its dangers. The very love of children can lead to self-love, self-important possessiveness, and a rejection of one of the central premises of Rosh HaShanah and the penitential season.

That central premise, difficult to absorb, is the renouncing of absolute ownership over anything in our lives. Jews repeat throughout the season: *Haneshamah lakh vehaguf shelakh,* "The soul is Yours and the body is Yours." From a Jewish perspective, our lives are not our own. To acknowledge this is the first step toward repentance and repair.

Nor is that all. If our lives are not our own, neither are the lives of our children, lives more precious to us than our own. That is the key lesson brought home in the reading from the prophets on the first day of Rosh HaShanah when, her prayers answered, the formerly childless Hannah gives birth to a son and names him Samuel (in Hebrew, Shmuel). In a characteristic bit of biblical wordplay, Hannah explains her reason for the name: *Ki meHashem she'iltiv*. Although this is often translated as "because I asked God for him," the proper translation, Rabbi Joseph Soloveitchik suggested, is "because I have *borrowed* him from God" (I Sam. 1:20). In then consecrating Samuel to the service of God, Hannah recognized the great truth: our children are not so much "owned" by us as on loan to us as their custodians and guardians on behalf of God.

Which brings us to the readings on the second day. If the first day's readings remind us of our capacity as parents to imitate God's love for us even as we must always remain mindful of our children's "borrowed" state, the second day's readings offer extreme instances of the rule.

First comes the intensely disturbing Torah story known in Hebrew as the *Akeidah*, "the binding," and in English traditionally referred to as the Sacrifice of Isaac, the only child of Abraham and Sarah. Here is God's instruction to Abraham, in the King James Version's unforgettably haunting translation:

> Take now thy son, thine only son Isaac, whom thou lovest, and get thee into the land of Moriah; and offer him there for a burnt offering upon one of the mountains which I will tell thee of. (Gen. 22:2)

The images and themes of this biblical story also pervade the Rosh HaShanah liturgy. According to our prayer books, one of the biblical names for Rosh HaShanah, Yom HaZikaron, "The Day of Remembrance," is a reference to God as the One who remembers the promises made to Abraham after the trauma of the *Akeidah*. That, indeed, was surely one of the prime reasons in later Jewish history for the preferred shofar to become not merely an animal horn but, specifically, a ram's horn: as a reminder of the twisted appendage of the ram caught in a thicket, the animal that in Genesis serves as the sacrificial replacement for the son who was restored to his father.

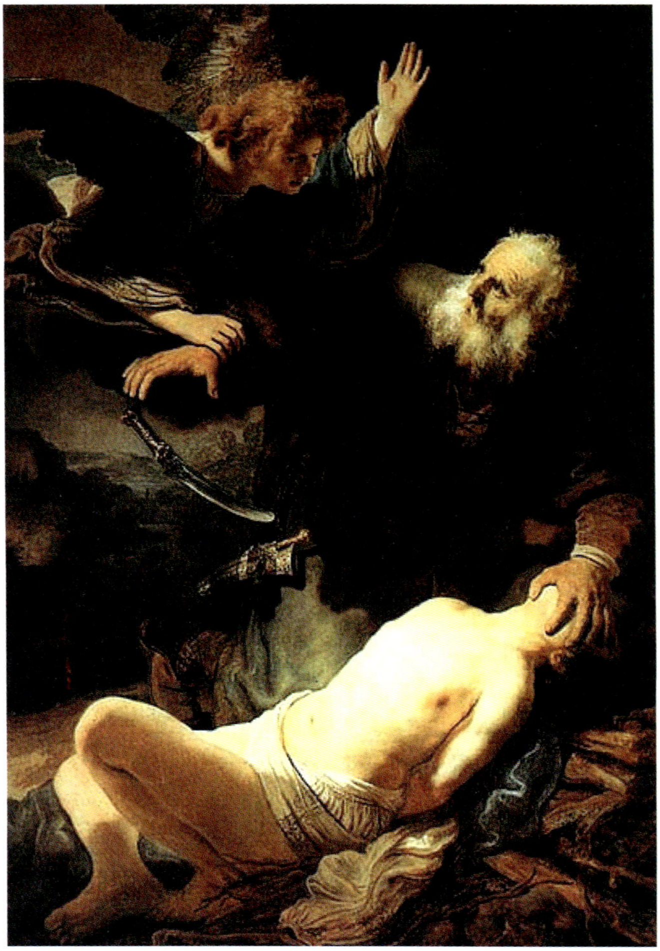

▲ *The Sacrifice of Isaac,* Rembrandt van Rijn

Every Sephardi and Mizraḥi Jew knows, or knows of, *Eit Shaarei Ratzon,* "The Gates of [God's] Will," a twelfth-century liturgical poem by Judah ben Samuel ibn Abbas, whose dramatic verses are sung immediately prior to blowing the shofar on Rosh HaShanah. The rhymed and agonizingly suspenseful six-line stanzas of *Eit Shaarei Ratzon* retell the entire story of the *Akeidah,* from God's first instruction to Abraham till the last-minute heavenly reprieve. The poem became the Sephardi version of the *Untaneh Tokef* – a verse prayer on the theme of divine judgment that instantly conjures up the advent of the new year.

And just as the first theme of Rosh HaShanah – creation – is enhanced by the second theme – the birth of children – so, too, are both themes, and especially the second, enhanced by the third: the *Akeidah*.

A contemporary anecdote may help illustrate what is entailed here. Once, on a Friday morning in London, Rabbi Sacks accompanied Penelope Leach, a prominent British child psychologist, on a visit to a Jewish primary school. There she witnessed children play-acting the rituals of the Shabbat meal that, as Friday evening fell, would take place in their homes. Boys blessed the wine, girls kindled candles, Sabbath songs were sung.

Leach was struck by everything she saw, but was enthralled by one moment in particular: the children's reenactment of a tradition in many Jewish homes in which, before the Sabbath meal begins, the father extends his hands over the head of each child and intones a brief one-sentence blessing, varied only slightly according to whether the child is a boy or a girl and followed by the so-called priestly blessing from the book of Numbers: "May the Lord bless you and keep you. May the Lord cause His Presence to shine upon you and grace you. May the Lord turn with favor to you, and give you peace" (6:24–26).

Moved by this dramatic example of the centrality of family life in traditional Judaism, Leach, as Rabbi Sacks reports, marveled at "the five-year-old mother and father blessing the five-year-old children with the five-year-old grandparents looking on."

> "May the Lord bless you and keep you. May the Lord cause His Presence to shine upon you and grace you. May the Lord turn with favor to you, and give you peace" (Numbers 6:24–26).

Friday Evening Blessing, Moritz Daniel Oppenheim

The ritual of Jewish parents blessing their children is indeed a marvel, and a very moving one. But it is easily misconstrued. The standard form of showing love to our children is physical, through an embrace that draws them close to us; as an action, it is at once protective and possessive. By contrast, the biblical words stress not the bond between parent and child but rather the bond between each child and God. Blessing our children by extending our hands sets them apart, acknowledging that, like us, they belong to Someone other than ourselves.

In the Torah, the one ritual act comparable to this blessing has to do with Temple sacrifice. As the book of Leviticus informs us, an Israelite worshipper making an offering of an animal in the Temple prefaces the ritual by placing his hands on the animal's head, thereby renouncing his own claim and dedicating the offering to God: "And he shall place his hands on the head of the burnt offering, and it shall be accepted as an atonement for him" (1:4).

In this sense, one might say that the *Akeidah* is symbolically recreated every Friday evening in many Jewish homes all over the world. When parents place their hands on their children's heads as their ancestors did over offerings in Jerusalem millennia ago, a sacred familial experience recalls one of the most petrifying tales ever told about parent and child.

This point was made by Rabbi Soloveitchik in a correspondence with a Catholic priest in the 1950s. At the heart of the religious worldview, he suggested, is the idea that man is merely "a guardian in whose care the works of God have been placed as a precious charge." And this is especially true of children, "the greatest and most precious charge," concerning whom the "irrevocable though bitter truth" is that they are not ours. For Abraham to deserve fatherhood, he too, at the *Akeidah,* had to prove his acceptance of that same bitter, irrevocable truth. Today, as Rabbi Soloveitchik put it, "parents must always remain aware that it is only through God's infinite grace that this infant has been returned to them in sacred trust."[2]

For many modern Jews, the story of the *Akeidah* is an embarrassing anachronism, and the descriptions of animal sacrifice in Leviticus are seen as utterly irrelevant to our lives. But are they? As the prominent ethicist Leon Kass has noted, many parents devote their children to "some 'god' or other, to Mammon or Molech, to honor or money, to pleasure or power, or, worse, to no god at all." A true father and mother, by contrast, in devoting their children only to godly ways, recognize that parenthood is a duty and not a right, and that children are "a gift and a blessing from God."[3]

And this makes the third and last theme the most relevant of all to an affluent age that has lavished love on children, coddled and protected them, denied them little or nothing, and (as Senator Ben Sasse has noted in his book *The Vanishing American Adult*) produced a generation of young people too often locked in perpetual adolescence. Is it not possible that what we need is less embracing and more blessing, less possession and more consecration? Every parent would prefer to consign the *Akeidah* story to oblivion, and yet, especially today, the *Akeidah,* the shofar, and the liturgy of Rosh HaShanah continue to call out to us.

These, then, are three of the central themes of this day. First: God is our King and our Creator. Second: It is in imitation of divine creation that Jews bring children into this world. Third: These children, though created by us, are not owned by us; we are their custodians, and our most important role is to raise them to moral adulthood so that they in turn can, like Abraham millennia ago, come to comprehend God as Creator and partner with Him in becoming creators of families of their own.

I promised three themes. But they are complemented, finally, by a fourth that is integrally connected with them and by no means exclusive to Rosh HaShanah but is integrally connected with it and with the other three themes. And that is the theme sounded with exquisite appropriateness in the prophetic reading for the second day, immediately after the reading of the *Akeidah*. Voiced by God through the prophet Jeremiah, it is a thrilling vision of consolation and restoration that, in emotionally charged and vivid imagery, reiterates the certain promise of His unbreakable love for His people – "My firstborn" (31:9), for whom "My heart yearns" (v. 20) – and, no matter what Israel might do to incur God's anger, the no-less-certain promise of their redemption: "Hear the word of the Lord, O ye nations, and declare it in the isles afar off, and say, 'He that scattered Israel will gather him, and keep him as a shepherd his flock'" (v. 10).

It is the combination of all four of these themes that once again presents a key to the endurance and eternity of the Jewish people.

CHAPTER TWO
Yom Kippur

Moses Bringing the Tablets of the Law, John Rogers Herbert

In the Palace of Westminster, the magnificent edifice in London where the two Houses of Parliament meet, the main chamber in the House of Lords stands out for its exquisite tapestries and the gilded royal throne set aside for the reigning monarch.

But right next door to the main chamber is another grand room, dominated by a massive canvas by the nineteenth-century British artist John Rogers Herbert depicting the prophet Moses as he descends Mount Sinai with the two tablets of the Law. Aptly named the "Moses Room," this chamber is utilized by the lords for committee meetings. It is also where newly appointed members don their ermine-embroidered cloaks before entering the main chamber for their ceremonial swearing-in.

Praying in the Synagogue on Yom Kippur, Maurycy Gottlieb

In 1998, Immanuel Jakobovits, the chief rabbi of the British Commonwealth, was made a life peer of the realm. Now a baron, he found himself in the Moses Room preparing to enter the House of Lords as a new member when an official attending him is reported to have said, "You know, Chief Rabbi, you're the first rabbi to be honored in this building." Gesturing at the painting of Moses, Rabbi Jakobovits replied something to the effect of: "No, actually, I'm the second rabbi to be honored here."

Herbert's painting does not show that earlier "rabbi" bringing down the first set of tablets. Nor does it show him quickly smashing them in anger at the Israelites' worship of the Golden Calf. Rather, it captures the scene several months later as Moses brings a second set of tablets. Indeed, the figure of Moses is not even the work's most striking element. Much of the canvas is devoted to the crowd of repentant Israelites waiting anxiously at the foot of Sinai to greet their leader.

And they have ample reason to be anxious: In response to the sin of the Golden Calf, God had announced that He would no longer dwell among the Jewish people. Has He now forgiven them? Might the covenant, shattered by their wanton behavior, have been renewed, the gift of God's presence granted once more? On their faces as Moses appears with the second tablets is, indeed, an expression of deep relief.

According to Jewish tradition, this moment, the descent from Sinai of Moses proclaiming God's forgiveness, took place on the tenth day of the Hebrew month of Tishrei, thereby establishing that day forevermore as Yom Kippur, a day of fasting, human contrition, and atonement, the day on which, beseeching His mercy, we all stand before God as humans who have failed to live up to our moral and spiritual potential.

For us humans, there are thus two aspects to this day. As the theologian Michael Wyschogrod once remarked, Jews may not believe in original sin, but no one ever walks into a synagogue on Yom Kippur and says: God, give me exactly what I deserve. We depend, rather, on a real element of divine benevolence and compassion. But that is on the one hand. On the other hand, Jewish thought, Jewish law, and the day's Jewish liturgy emphasize the irreplaceable role that must be played by human commitment, human will, and the human effort to repent, to right wrongs, and to restore our relationship not only with God but also with our fellow humans.

And here the giving of the second set of tablets at Sinai imparts a critical lesson. As many have noted, the first set was created entirely by God. But the second set, the set given on the tenth of Tishrei, was made by man. *Pesol lekha shenei luḥot avanim,* Moses is told by the Almighty – "Carve *for yourself* two tablets of stone" (Ex. 34:1, emphasis added). On this second set, painstakingly crafted through human effort, God re-inscribes the words of the Decalogue.

What can this mean? The first set, brought miraculously into being by the fiery finger of God Himself, lasted all of several minutes before being smashed by a furious Moses at the foot of the mountain. The second set, manufactured through the laborious exertions of the octogenarian leader himself, lasted forever. On Yom Kippur, in addition to hoping for divine forgiveness, we posit our capacity as human beings to carve our lives anew, to overcome our failings, fix our flaws, restore our relationships, and re-sculpt our character.

But how? What has gone missing from our worldview, and gone lacking in our moral capacities? What about God have we unlearned, and how are we to become who we are meant to be?

To those last questions, the answer conveyed again and again throughout the long day's liturgy lies in the act known as *vidui*, confession. It is not enough to regret past actions; it does not suffice to feel bad about our sins or to promise ourselves we'll do better. Instead, standing in the presence of the Almighty, we recount aloud our sinful actions and assume our responsibility for them.

At the center of prayer on Yom Kippur are two forms of verbal confession. One is known by its first two words, *Al ḥeit*, "For the sin…." Proceeding in couplets through the twenty-two letters of the Hebrew alphabet, it consists of a long litany of named transgressions, each of which begins, "For the sin that we have committed before You" – by, for example, failing to honor our parents, behaving dishonestly in our business dealings, speaking falsely, and so forth. Yet, lengthy as it is, the list is not meant to be exhaustive. Each of us is also meant to think about specific wrongs we have committed in the past year and of which we are ashamed, and to confess them to God.

The second type of confession, known by its first word as *Ashamnu*, "We are guilty," is a more general proclamation. It is prefaced by a plea: Do not think, God, that we are such incorrigible reprobates as to claim that we are actually righteous and innocent. Rather, in truth we are guilty – guilty as charged. An itemized list of these charges again follows through the letters of the Hebrew alphabet: *Ashamnu, bagadnu, gazalnu, dibarnu dofi....* "We are guilty, we have dealt treacherously, we have robbed, we have slandered, we have been perverse, we have wrought wickedness...we have gone astray, we have led others astray."

Vidui, confession in these two forms, constitutes the centerpiece of the traditional prayers on Yom Kippur, a day on which exceptionally large numbers of Jews attend synagogue services. And herein lies a great irony, for these confessions embody two themes that in today's environment are profoundly countercultural: the pervasive presence of God as the supreme judge of human virtue and sinfulness, and the radical freedom of man.

Before explicating the point, let's illustrate it. Of the four readings from Scripture on Yom Kippur, two each in the morning and afternoon, the fourth and final one is the entire book of the prophet Jonah. The story is famous; its significance is less well known or appreciated.

God commands the prophet to inform a city named Nineveh that its sinfulness has reached a point of no return and will result in its certain and imminent destruction. Knowing, however, God's propensity for forgiveness, and worried that his prophetic message will inspire the Ninevites to repent and thereby invalidate his mission and disgrace him as a prophet, Jonah flees aboard a boat. When the vessel is struck by a fierce storm, the sailors attempt to puzzle out the source of their ill fortune. For the English translation we again turn to the incomparable King James Version:

Jonah and the Whale, Carlo Antonio Tavella

> And they said every one to his fellow, "Come, let us cast lots, that we may know for whose cause this evil is upon us." So they cast lots, and the lot fell upon Jonah. Then said they unto him, "Tell us, we pray thee, for whose cause this evil is upon us; what is thine occupation? And whence comest thou? What is thy country? And of what people art thou?" And he said unto them, "I am a Hebrew; and I fear the Lord, the God of heaven, which hath made the sea and the dry land." Then were the men exceedingly afraid, and said unto him, "Why hast thou done this?" For the men knew that he fled from the presence of the Lord, because he had told them. (Jonah 1:7–10)

They knew? Because he had told them? If they knew from the beginning that the prophet was fleeing from God, why now were they mystified as to the cause of the storm, and why, when the lot fell on Jonah, did they need to learn his biography?

The passage is puzzling, but we should observe that Jonah has not answered all of the sailors' questions about his identity. He has supplied only one datum: *Ivri anokhi*, "I am a Hebrew." But that is evidently enough – for, though often overlooked, the fact is that "Hebrew" is not merely an ethnic but also a theological term, and its message in Jonah's story is central to Yom Kippur.

In the ancient Near East, as Rabbi Yoel Bin-Nun has pointed out, most people believed in territorial divinities: local gods who exercised tyrannical rule over a country's inhabitants but were powerless beyond its borders. From the gods' point of view, an area that was not part of any particular realm was no-man's-land, a place where one could do as one pleased.

In the Bible, by contrast, the God of the Hebrews is a God whose power is everywhere. A hint lies in the very term "Hebrew," which derives from the verb *la'avor*, to cross over. Abraham is the first to be called *ivri*, no doubt because he crossed over to the land of Canaan from the other side of the Jordan. The theological corollary? Abraham crossed over because the God who addressed him in Mesopotamia told him to cross over, assuring him that He would be with him on the other side. The Hebrew name *ivri* thus connotes one who asserts that no place on earth is devoid of God's presence and providence.

Turning back now to the story of the fleeing prophet: It would seem that Jonah told his fellow sailors from the start that he was seeking to flee his God. If this had not disturbed them, it was because they were sailing into international waters where the territorial gods had no power. Then, as the storm hits, each cries out to his own god – in the vain hope, perhaps, that the various deities thus summoned might mount a joint rescue operation. When that fails, and when the lot falls on Jonah, they demand to know who he *really* is. When he tells them, the stunned sailors finally grasp the true gravity of their situation: The Hebrews' divinity is none other than the "God of heaven, who hath made the sea and the dry land." He is, in short, everywhere.

This is the same realization that confession on Yom Kippur is meant to provoke in *us*. In standing before God and confessing to particular sins, we say, repeatedly: *Al ḥeit sheḥatanu lefanekha,* "We acknowledge and confess this particular sin that we committed before *You*." In sinning, we not only violate God's law and disobey His command, we are insensitive to His presence; we act as if He weren't there at all. The source of all of our sins is this insensitivity – which is why it does not suffice merely to regret what we did; we must confess to God personally, facing Him as if facing a friend, personally conversing with the One Who is everywhere. Indeed, linguistically, the Hebrew word for sin – *aveira* – is linked to *ivri*. Its root similarly means to cross over, to enter a realm of our lives where we act as if God were non-existent; it is to gerrymander the divine out of our daily experience.

In Jonah, the book and the person, the essence of Jewish belief is succinctly and powerfully summarized. *Ivri anokhi!* God is to be found anywhere, at any time. And confession, as the book of Jonah again teaches, is the first step toward reorienting our relationship with God – not in order to inform Him what we have done but in order to bring home to ourselves that He was there when we did it.

Yom Kippur is the climax of the *Yamim Noraim*, usually translated as High Holy Days but more appropriately rendered as fearsome and awesome days, fearsome and awesome not because of our terror of punishment but rather because on these days we strive to achieve a full realization of the presence of God.

This realization, today, is very difficult to achieve, seeming as it does to require a "religious" event – an epiphany – outside the sphere of our control. Indeed, applying the modern term "religious" to such an experience already implies that there are some spheres of life where God's presence is made manifest and others where it is absent. In that respect, our time is not so different from Jonah's. We all gerrymander God from parts of our life.

Against that background, it might help to be reminded of the testimony to the contrary offered by some of the greatest Jewish heroes of our time. Think, for instance, of the Soviet "refusenik" Natan Sharansky, trapped in an evil Communist empire insistently proclaiming that there is no God and persecuting any who dared think or act otherwise. Released at last from the prison camp to which he had been sentenced on trumped-up charges, Sharansky would title his memoir *Fear No Evil*, a reference to King David's thrilling assertion of faith: "Though I walk in the valley of the shadow of death, I will fear no evil, for Thou art with me!" (Ps. 23:4). Sharansky writes:

> When I first came across the concept of *yirat shamayim* (the fear or awe of heaven, i.e., God), I automatically understood it as referring to the fear of God's punishment for our sins. But as I read the Psalms it became harder to maintain this narrow, utilitarian understanding of these words. Why had I refused to enter into any discussions with the KGB after my trial? … Why was it so important for me not to take one step back toward that servile life I had once led?[1]

The answer, for Sharansky, lay in another biblical verse: "The fear of God is the beginning of wisdom" (Prov. 9:10). For him,

> these words seemed to be a natural summation of long years of spiritual search.... Does it really matter where this religious feeling stems from....? For me, the important thing is that this feeling really does exist, that I sense its force and power over me, that it influences my deeds and my life, and that for ten years it has linked me with [my wife] Avital more concretely than any letters.[2]

Confession, then, involves an acknowledgement of God's presence in our lives. But it also teaches us something important about ourselves. And here we turn to the *ashamnu* ("we have sinned, we are guilty") version of the *vidui*, with its emphasis less on specific sins than on our moral condition.

The source of this confessional mode can be found in Genesis in the tale of Joseph's brothers, whose jealous hatred of their sibling led them to seize him, to sell him literally down the river, and to lie to their father about the reason for his disappearance. Years later, they find themselves being hectored and persecuted by the great vizier of Egypt – who is, unbeknownst to them, the very same brother they had so egregiously wronged. Pondering why God has brought this humiliation upon them, they engage in a process of moral reflection that ultimately, after further twists and turns of the plot, results in the brothers' repentance, in the vizier's revealing himself to them as their brother, and in his forgiveness of their treatment of him:

> Then they said to one another, "But in truth, we are guilty concerning our brother, in that we saw the distress of his soul, when he besought us and we would not listen; therefore is this distress come upon us." (Gen. 42:21)

Aval asheimim anaḥnu – "But in truth, we are guilty." The confession is prefaced by the word "but," as if some of them had sought to excuse their actions. And in fact, for days after having sold Joseph into slavery, the brothers talking among themselves sought for some excuse to mitigate their misdeed. It is to these shameful exculpatory thoughts that they now confess in their "But in truth we are guilty." In his enslavement, while they went scot-free, lay their culpability.

This biblical approach to sin and redemption is irreconcilable with either ancient paganism or modern secular materialism; for each, man is essentially unfree, and therefore not truly responsible. In the biblical age, as all of Jacob's children were well aware, countless cultures proclaimed that one's actions were controlled by the planets, and one's fate by the stars. In the modern age, no lesser a figure than Albert Einstein once remarked: "I know that, philosophically, a murderer is not responsible for his crime," adding, lamely, "but I prefer not to take tea with him."

In this respect, the modern materialist is akin to the pagan of old in that, as the physicist Stephen M. Barr has put it, the materialist

> ends up subjecting man to the subhuman. The pagan said that his actions were controlled by the orbits of the planets and stars, the materialist says they are controlled by the orbits of the electrons in his brain.... The pagan spoke of fate, the materialist speaks of physical determinism.[3]

To such an approach, the brothers' confession makes a ringing reply: "We are free, *and* we are guilty."

On Yom Kippur, this is what we, too, proclaim. One cannot utter the central proclamation, *Ashamnu, "We are guilty,"* without believing in human freedom. Thus, Moses Maimonides (1138–1204) in his code of Jewish law, the *Mishneh Torah,* devotes an entire chapter of his discussion of Yom Kippur and repentance to defending the philosophical notion of free will against all detractors. The essence:

> The ability is given to every human being. If he wishes to turn himself to the righteous path, he has that ability, and if he wishes to turn toward evil, he has *that* ability.[4]

Just as one cannot confess to guilt without free will, there is no Yom Kippur without the Jewish doctrine of human freedom.

And just as the liturgy of Yom Kippur is in tension with our time in terms of its theology, so too is it deeply countercultural in its moral anthropology. For we live today in an age and culture of victimhood, where bad things happen to us not through our seeming irresponsibility or immorality but because of external factors beyond our control, and where every step is taken to protect us in a cocoon of protective caution and relieve of us of responsibility. That is why, writes George Will,

> in the home of the free and the land of the brave you can buy a five-inch fishing lure with a warning label on it that says "harmful if swallowed." You can buy a letter opener that says "safety goggles recommended." You can buy a clothes iron that says on it "warning: do not iron clothes on body." You can buy a child's stroller that says "remove child before folding." [5]

But in truth we *are* responsible, precisely because we are free – and it is this freedom that we invoke when in prayer after prayer on Yom Kippur we proclaim our own guilt. *Ashamnu.* And this same freedom means that *ashamnu* has another, extraordinary implication. If we are free, then, on the one hand, we are responsible, at fault for our flaws. On the other hand, if we are truly free, we are able to change, to progress, to repent, to correct, to make things right.

> "It is this freedom that we invoke when, in prayer after prayer on Yom Kippur, we proclaim our own guilt."

Here Judaism parts with another prominent religious approach to man. In the literature of some faiths, repentance is described as the mere acknowledgment of moral wretchedness: Man in this world is a fallen creature, deservedly damned, a rebellious enemy of God. Incapable of fixing his own flaws, he must acknowledge his guilt and throw himself at God's mercy. The great religious scholar and philosopher C.S. Lewis, in *Mere Christianity*, argues that

> [f]allen man is not simply an imperfect creature who needs improvement: he is a rebel who must lay down his arms.... This process of surrender is what Christians call repentance.... It means killing part of yourself, undergoing a kind of death.[6]

For Lewis, this is what Jesus does on our behalf. But for Jewish religious literature, repentance is something very different. Man is not a wretched rebel, an enemy of God. Man truly is, to borrow from Lewis, "an imperfect creature who needs improvement,"[7] and is capable of achieving that improvement through his own effort. Rather than a humbling surrender, repentance is a triumph of the human spirit. God demands repentance of us, in the certainty that we are capable of achieving it through an exercise of strength of which we may not even have been aware. For Judaism, Rabbi Soloveitchik writes, "Man's task in the world is to transform a passive existence into an active existence, an existence of compulsion into an existence replete with a powerful will, with resourcefulness, daring, and imagination."[8]

> "*Teshuvah* can begin only by truly understanding what we are capable of, and by realizing that we have not lived up to those capabilities."

Every step in the process of *teshuvah*, of "return" – of repenting our past misdeeds and changing our ways – can begin only by truly understanding what we are capable of, and by realizing that we have not lived up to those capabilities. We can accept responsibility for everything that we have done wrong only by saying that we *failed* to do that which was perfectly in our power *to* do.

It is for this reason that some Jewish communities have had the custom of proclaiming *Ashamnu* – "We are guilty" not in sadness but in joy. For there is no guilt without freedom, and as a frustrated Jonah learns following Nineveh's repentance, the very freedom that allows for guilt also allows for change, for improvement. To know that we are guilty of not doing better is to know that we could have done better, and to know that we could have done better is to affirm that we *can* do better.

On one of my visits to the Moses Room of the House of Lords, studying John Rogers Herbert's depiction of the first Yom Kippur, I noticed something that I'd missed earlier. In this painting, unlike in most artistic presentations of the tale, the tablets borne by Moses are not finely carved; their edges are instead rough and jagged. The artist had understood that these were the tablets painstakingly chiseled by Moses himself. They look exactly as what they were: man-made.

We human tablets of Yom Kippur are imperfect, but also gifted with powerful potential. We are the tablets, and as much as Yom Kippur informs us about God, it also informs us about ourselves. To those who insist that humans are a bundle of uncontrollable, irrepressible urges, Judaism asserts that we are free. To those who submit that humans are inherently evil, unable to repent on their own – so sinful that they must be saved from themselves – Judaism submits that (in Rabbi Soloveitchik's phrasing) man is born an object and dies an object but can live as a subject. Yom Kippur comes every year, it will be needed every year, and still, year after year, it proclaims its faith in our moral capacity. It asserts, idealistically but realistically, critically but optimistically, that mankind is not inherently good, but is capable of goodness.

In this connection, finally, one of my all-time favorite paintings is Rembrandt's stunning 1659 portrait of Moses holding the tablets of the law aloft. In the museum in Berlin where it hangs, its title has long been given as *Moses zerschmettert die Gesetzsestafeln*, "Moses Shatters the Tablets of the Law," and so it is also habitually referred to by others. According to the museum's interpretation, Rembrandt is depicting the moment of Israel's greatest failure.

But the museum's title is controversial and probably mistaken. Moses does not look angry; extraordinary light pours forth from his

Moses zerschmettert die Gesetzestafeln (Moses Shatters the Tablets of the Law), Rembrandt van Rijn

face. Many scholars have therefore persuasively argued that Rembrandt in this image has offered us not the destruction of the first set of tablets but – like John Rogers Herbert three centuries later – the restoration of the second: the tablets carved by Moses himself.

Here, in what I have called the most Jewish painting of all time, Rembrandt gives us the first Yom Kippur in history: the Yom Kippur that insists we are imperfect, a work in progress, but therefore all the more extraordinary for having been carved by the effort of man. May the tablets honored in Britain in the House of Lords be honored by each of us, in our confessions and prayers, in whatever house of the Lord we find ourselves on Yom Kippur, this year or any year.

Chapter Three
Sukkot

Of all the holidays on the Jewish calendar, Sukkot, the biblical "Festival of Booths," must surely seem the one most out of place in today's world. Dwelling in a sukkah (hut)? Hoisting palm fronds aloft and waving them about? The thought of otherwise normal-seeming human beings freely choosing to conduct themselves, however briefly, in so blatantly primitive a manner must strike the onlooker as bewildering at best, if not downright inconceivable.

In this connection, let me begin by citing my favorite Sukkot tale, as related by the travel writer Devorah Klein Lev-Tov. It seems that the family of Lev-Tov's mother, having recently left the city of Detroit for the suburbs, found itself "huddled in the sukkah on a chilly Friday night, eating bowls of warm stew" – when, suddenly,

> two men with guns burst in demanding money, an increasingly common occurrence in the Detroit area at the time. My mother and her family, having no money with them because it was both Shabbat and a holiday, just stared at the men, unsure of what to do next. As the men stared back, one looked at his companion and said, "I don't think these people have anything. They're sitting in a hut eating beans! They've got less than we do!" And with that, they left, leaving my mother and her family stunned and grateful.[1]

What, then, *is* this holiday, and what should it mean to us? We'll proceed in stages, first dealing with the biblical festival as it was meant to be lived in the land of Israel, then turning to the story of Sukkot through the centuries of exile, and finally returning to Sukkot today with the Jewish people restored to its land. Only through understanding what Sukkot was can we appreciate what it is – and why a holiday that seems so incongruous in today's day and age, even to would-be burglars, speaks so profoundly to the moral and spiritual challenges of our own time.

In the Bible, Sukkot is referred to as *Ḥag Ha'asif*, a seven-day "harvest festival" in the Holy Land that occurs just before the onset of the rainy season; it is capped by an "Eighth Day of Assembly" – that is, the holiday of Shemini Atzeret – with its special prayer for rain. For Sukkot itself, two central rituals are ordained, and both have continued to be faithfully observed throughout the ages and around the globe.

The first is to spend all seven days dwelling – that is, eating, drinking, sleeping – in a sukkah, a made-to-order shack or "booth." This practice, we are informed, serves as a remembrance of the Israelites' wandering in the desert after the Exodus from Egypt, deprived of any permanent homes for their shelter. The second ritual centers on taking specimens of what are known as the *arba minim*, the land of Israel's "four types" or agricultural species – a frond of the date palm, *lulav*; a citron, *etrog*; and branches of myrtle and willow, *hadasim* and *aravot* – and with them, "rejoicing in the presence of God for seven days." These rituals, spelled out in the book of Leviticus, can at least in part be performed anywhere, but ideally are prescribed to take place in the precincts of the Temple in Jerusalem (23:39–42).

> "[Sukkot] is the original Thanksgiving – the holiday on which we are intended to thank God for what we have."

As a harvest festival, Sukkot is thus essentially a Jewish thanksgiving. More properly, it is the *original* Thanksgiving – the holiday on which we are intended to thank God for what we have while also, at moments, beseeching God to grant abundant rain and harvests in the coming year. The four species represent the agriculture and irrigation of the land of Israel, and the biblical verses recited while raising and clutching them are the biblical psalms of thanksgiving, or Hallel (Ps. 113–118).

Foremost among the species is the palm frond, meant to be taken specifically from a date palm. And little wonder: The Holy Land was known for its flourishing palm trees, whole forests of which covered the Jordan River valley, and for the exceptional quality of the dates themselves. When the Bible calls the land of Israel a land of milk and honey, the latter term refers to honey not from bees but from dates: a supreme symbol of the harvest and thus, of the nation of Israel itself.

Sukkot, in other words, is intended for a people living in an agrarian society and in its own land; it is a holiday for a nation-state engaged closely with nature. But in that engagement there lurk a number of potential spiritual pitfalls. One is the *worship* of nature – that is, paganism. Another is hubris, arrogance, or the worship of self. The biblical version of the holiday is intended to counter these stumbling blocks.

But what exactly do we mean by nature? For us, nature is something we find upon leaving the city and going to "the country." But as C.S. Lewis notes in his book *Reflection on the Psalms* (1958), the word "nature," in our sense, does not actually exist in the Hebrew Bible. For people living in the biblical age, nature was not something separate from the world in which they found themselves. As water is to a fish, nature *was* the world in which they found themselves.

In this regard, Lewis remarks, the difference between biblical Judaism and paganism is not merely the difference between one God versus many gods. An equally important point of difference centers on the issue of whether nature is created by God or is itself divine.

In the ancient Near East, creation – the idea that God, in the beginning, created heaven and earth – was largely unheard of. Lewis writes:

> I suspect that many people [today] assume that some clear doctrine of creation underlies all religions: that in paganism the gods, or one of the gods, usually

> created the world, and even that religions normally begin by answering the question, "Who made the world?" In reality, [however,] creation, in any unambiguous sense, seems to be a surprisingly rare doctrine, and when stories about it occur in paganism they are often religiously unimportant.... In one Egyptian story a god called Atum came up out of the water and, being apparently a hermaphrodite, begot and bore the two next gods; after that, things could develop. In another, the whole senate of the gods came up out of Nun, the Deep....[2]

And so forth. The point, Lewis tells us, is not that these and other myths – he adduces examples from Babylonian, Greek, and Norse traditions – are crude. What's most interesting is not their explanations for nature but the questions they are not even asking. To illustrate this, Lewis adduces the example of a man who

> has arrived ten minutes late to Shakespeare's *Macbeth* and asks what has happened so far. He might be properly answered, say, with the words: "Oh, first three witches came in, and then there was a scene between an old king and a wounded soldier." That is the sort of question the myths are in fact answering. But the very different question: "How does a play originate? Does it write itself? Do the actors make it up as they go along? Or is there someone – not on the stage, not like the people on the stage – someone we don't see – who invented it all and caused it to be?"[3]

As Lewis writes, such questions are rarely either asked or answered by any of the pagan civilizations. But these are precisely the questions that Jews do ask – and answer. Biblical Israel is interested not only in what is happening "onstage" but also in who made the stage and who wrote the play. When the Bible opens by giving us the answer – "In the beginning God created the heaven and the earth" – nature, now shorn of any intrinsic divinity of its own, can be seen as a masterpiece *by* the Almighty: "The heavens proclaim the glory of God" (Ps. 19:1).

This was a revolution. And yet, even for biblical Israel, the temptation to worship nature remained ever-present. And that is where Sukkot enters the picture, as a method of reorienting the Israelite mind and ensuring a proper perspective.

Precisely at harvest time – the central moment in the cycle of nature – when veneration of nature itself would loom most saliently in the imagination, Israelite farmers were commanded to sit in a sukkah and remember the Exodus – when God, blotting out the sun and splitting the sea, made manifest His absolute power simultaneously over nature and over Egypt's gods. Taking the four species of their harvest in their hands, the Israelite farmers would praise the Creator of nature, seeing in it not gods but the gift of God.

Still, even if nature had been de-divinized, a correlative danger loomed: that the Israelites, having harnessed nature by creating and harvesting crops, would forget the divine and ascribe the achievement to themselves. That is the central concern of the book of Deuteronomy: namely, that after entering the land, working it, planting, and reaping its crops, experiencing successful harvest after successful harvest, the Israelites who in the desert had sought sustenance only from God would forget that their harvest was itself God's benevolent bounty.

Were one to summarize Deuteronomy's message to the Israelites about to enter the land, wrote Rabbi Jonathan Sacks, it would go like this:

> For forty years, you and your parents wandered in the wilderness.... Only by a series of miracles did you have anything to eat or drink. Now you have reached the brink of the promised land. You think this will be the end of your challenges. On the contrary, it is here that the challenge will begin, and it will be the hardest challenge of all because it will not look like a challenge, but "when you eat and are satisfied, when all you have is multiplied, then beware lest your heart become proud and you forget God" (8:11).[4]

Here, Rabbi Sacks notes, Moses "gives voice to the most counterintuitive of messages: that one of the greatest of challenges is not servitude but freedom, not poverty but affluence. The paradox is that when we have most to thank God for, that is when we are in greatest danger of not thanking – nor even thinking of – God at all."[5]

The same paradox was invoked in the nineteenth century by Rabbi Samson Raphael Hirsch, who saw it as particularly acute at the moment of the *asif*, the ingathering of the harvest, when one would behold all that had been reaped and be tempted instinctively to attribute it entirely to one's own efforts, gifts, and power. It is as a corrective to that instinct that the Torah, in envisioning the scene, employs images of the arm and hand: "And you will say in your heart, 'My own power and the might of my own hand have won this abundance for me'" (Deut. 8:17).

At that moment, the farmer is most in need of bidding farewell to his field and ascending to Jerusalem to enter the Temple, to take in his arms and hands the botanical specimens symbolizing agricultural achievement, and with those arms and hands, which he might otherwise believe are the source of his strength, to transform symbols of

Letter by Shimon Bar Kokhba

Judea Capta coin

the harvest and embodiments of material success into symbols and embodiments of gratitude to God. Similarly, he is required to dwell for seven days not in the home he has built but in a booth reminiscent of the age when manna fell from heaven and water flowed from a rock, when Israel experienced every day its reliance on God's grace, just as the farmer relies on the same divine blessing for his bounty.

This, then, is Sukkot for biblical Israel, agrarian Israel, land-based Israel, nation-state Israel. We have one late glimpse of this Sukkot in an extraordinary letter discovered by the archeologist Yigal Yadin and written by no lesser a figure than the warrior Shimon Bar Kokhba in the very midst of his revolt against Rome (132–135 CE). Addressed by Bar Kokhba to "Yehudah, son of Menasheh, at Kiryat Arba," it says:

> I have delivered to you two donkeys for you to dispatch along with two men to Yehonatan, son of Ba'yan, and to Mesabalah so that they may pack up and deliver palm branches and citrons to the camp and to you. And you are to send additional persons from your place and let them bring you myrtle branches and willows. Prepare them, and deliver them to the camp, because the population is large. Fare well![6]

They did not fare well. The revolt failed, Bar Kokhba fell in battle, and in a cruel twist of fate, the date palm itself became utilized as a symbol of Jewish defeat. In proclaiming their conquest of Judea and their destruction of the Temple, the Romans minted coins featuring bound Jewish captives sitting under a date palm. Boldly emblazoned on the coins were the words *Iudea capta,* "Judea has been seized."

Over the subsequent centuries, Jews wandered the world, ultimately forced to abandon agriculture as a source of sustenance and living not in nature but in cities and towns, sometimes further enclosed within ghetto walls and gates.

But even in exile, Sukkot – the agricultural holiday of the Holy Land – continued to be observed. And this brings us to the second stage.

Wherever Jews were living throughout the ages, they sat in sukkot, and over the centuries, Sukkot itself came to symbolize not only the Israelites' wandering in the desert but also the wandering of Jews throughout the world, from place to place, never staying long, but always loyal to God. The Talmud codified as a matter of law, and Jewish thinkers stressed as a matter of theology, that the sukkah was to be considered a *dirat arai,* a temporary dwelling, one made to last for only seven days and even then not built high enough that it could mistakenly resemble a *dirat keva,* something permanent. Indeed, precisely because of its impermanence, a sukkah did not require a mezuzah, with its verses from the Torah, at the entrance. Instead, it embodied the very transience of Jewish existence, as temporary as the world in which Jews lived.

In one expression of this motif, most Jewish communities chose Sukkot as the holiday on which to read in synagogue the book of Ecclesiastes, *Kohelet,* which more than any other biblical book reflects on the changing of generations:

> For man also knoweth not his time; as the fishes that are taken in an evil net, and as the birds that are caught in the snare, even so are the sons of men snared in an evil time, when it falleth suddenly upon them. (9:12)

Death comes for us all – or, as Ecclesiastes famously begins: *Hevel havalim hakol havel,* which means not that all is futile but that all is transient. Sukkot became a time for reflecting on mortality, finitude, the temporary nature of life, of which the greatest symbol was the sukkah itself.

Echoing this thought, and expanding upon it, is the concluding statement in Paul Johnson's *A History of the Jews* (1987):

> The Jews were not just innovators, they were also exemplars and epitomizers of the human condition. The Jews were the emblem of homeless and vulnerable humanity. But is not the whole earth no more than a temporary transit camp?[7]

And yet, even as Sukkot took on the mark of mortality, it remained a time of celebration and gratitude – and indeed one of the *most* joyous holidays of the Jewish year: "You shall celebrate before the lord your God for seven days" (Lev. 23:41). Here rabbinic Judaism makes an astonishing philosophical leap: Not only is the experience of mortality reconcilable with the experience of joy, but the two are intertwined. Joy lies not in the denial of finitude but in its acknowledgment and realization. As Leon Kass has written, "Mortality makes life matter"; the same Jews from whom life has so often been "cruelly stolen" are the ones who toast *l'ḥayyim*, to life.

In the face of the finitude represented by the sukkah, Sukkot reminded Jews that they were an eternal people, that they were part of something much larger, and that their journey on earth began with Abraham's expedition to a specific land and would eventuate in a return to that land. All of this was embodied in the other ritual of the holiday: holding aloft the four species, symbols of the Holy Land, and singing psalms of joy and praise.

But how, during the long centuries of dispersion, could one *acquire* these embodied symbols of Israelite agriculture? It was not so difficult for Jews who lived in the Middle East or in Mediterranean societies. But for many Jews, spread throughout Europe, it was almost impossible; rabbinic rulings testify that often, a community's single palm frond would have to be re-used from year to year.

The most difficult of all to acquire was the *etrog*, the citron. And yet acquire it they did, often with households sharing among them the same small piece of fruit that nevertheless contained the power to link them not only spatially with Jews all over the world but temporally with Israelite farmers tilling the soil centuries earlier.

▲
Citron branch with buds, blossoms, and fruit

And here a fascinating union of Jewish morality, botanical science, and aesthetics reveals itself. While three of the four species are identified specifically, the citron is identified in the Torah only by the appellation *pri eitz hadar*, literally the "fruit of a beautiful [or: glorious] tree."

One might have expected that Jews, especially those facing difficulty in acquiring an *etrog*, would have concluded that any beautiful fruit could serve the ritualistic purpose. Instead, they stoutly adhered to the Jewish tradition that "the fruit of a glorious tree" referred to the *etrog* and only the *etrog*.

Is the *etrog* tree so glorious? Not according to Gil Marks's *Encyclopedia of Jewish Food* (2010):

> Historically, the citron, to put it mildly, was not a very useful plant. It was not the hardiest tree; its wood was not prized as lumber; it was not one of the tallest trees; it was vulnerable to cold temperatures; nor were its fruits considered a luxury food in the ancient world, like cherries and kumquats.[8]

If that is the case, what has made it such a coveted treasure? The answer, I think, lies in a fascinating botanical fact noted by Marks:

> The citron is unique in that it is the only tree that can flower and bear fruit throughout the year under proper conditions; it can also distinctively retain the fruit from one year to the next. Thus the citron is the only tree that can have buds, blossoms, and mature fruit at the same time.[9]

In other words, the *etrog* tree embodies for the Jews what is the most beautiful, the most glorious, the most profoundly Jewish value of all: continuity, the bond between generations. Indeed, the Talmud itself notes this in a pun on the word *hadar*: the "glory" of the *etrog* lies in the same fact to which Marks calls attention in his *Encyclopedia*: namely, that the fruit "dwells" (*dar*) on its tree from year to year (Sukkah 35a).

The tree, then, is the embodiment of endurance. Peoplehood, the link between generations, and the heritage of transmission are what enable Jews to achieve immortality. If the sukkah represents transience, the four species represent continuity, perpetuation, and eternity, of which the *etrog* tree is the sublime example. Or, as Leon Kass puts this same insight in another context:

> [I]n perpetuation, we send forth not just the seed of our bodies but also the bearer of our hopes, our truths, and those of our tradition. If our children are to flower, we need to sow them well and nurture them, cultivate them in rich and wholesome soil, clothe them in fine

> and decent opinions and mores, and direct them toward the highest light, to grow straight and tall – that they may take our place as we took that of those who planted us and made way for us, so that in time they, too, may make way and plant.[10]

Mortality and perpetuation, finitude and eternal peoplehood, all came together on this holiday. Whether in the desert sun of Yemen or the snowy drifts of Ukraine, Jews, none of whom had ever harvested anything, sat in their sukkot, sang the psalms of praise while holding the *lulav* and *etrog*, and were united across the world: an eternal people that exile and even the fact of death itself could not destroy.

Then, in stage three, the Jews returned to their land and a Jewish state was restored.

And that is not all that was restored. The Judean date palm, once the most famous symbol of a fruitful and fecund land, had long been extinct. The new state therefore set about to ensure the re-flourishing of the "land of milk and [date] honey." By means direct and indirect, aboveboard and surreptitious, Israel managed to import tens of thousands of date-palm saplings from other Near Eastern countries, not all of them well-disposed (to put it mildly) to the Jewish state. As the historian and neuroscientist Ari Zivotofsky of Bar-Ilan University summarizes the story: "These saplings 'mysteriously' turned up in Haifa and were used to rekindle the now very successful Israel date business in both the Arava [desert] and the Beit She'an valley."[11]

So it would be refreshing to report that all is well. Unfortunately, however, that is not the case. Yes, Sukkot today, with the Jewish people back in its land, speaks to us more than ever in its original accents and integrity. But throughout the world, and especially in the democratic West, the very ideas that the Bible once taught the world to reject – the worship of nature and of self – are sprouting once again.

Writing about the biblical psalms in the 1950s, C.S. Lewis mused that the instinct of pagan worship, with which the biblical Israelites had struggled, had been absent from Europe for a thousand years. He could not write that today. Even when nature is not embraced as divine in itself, we are too often lectured to venerate nature to a degree that supersedes the commands of God, the moral teachings of the Bible, and rabbinic Judaism with their emphasis on ritual and continuity.

One writer has actually argued in a Jewish newspaper that American Jews should altogether ditch the *lulav* and *etrog* as a favor to the environment:

> Each year, we produce a massive carbon footprint in the lead-up to Sukkot's celebration of abundance and its message to live more sustainably and more in concert with the seasons. I'm talking about the *lulav* and *etrog* – the palm frond, myrtle, willow, and citron that we Jews are commanded to bless during the holiday. As compost-friendly as they may be, they are flown in from Israel and shipped en masse to American Jewish communities that couldn't grow a palm tree or an *etrog* grove if they tried.
>
> But what luck: we're smack in the middle of the harvest season here in North America. We have maple and oak and aspen leaves. . . ; we have squash, apples, and pumpkins in abundance. So why are we still insisting on importing astronomically expensive produce and leaves from the Middle East rather than picking an apple off our trees, using maple and oak branches from our own yards, and shaking them the same way we do with the *lulav*?[12]

"Sukkot speaks to a nation that has rebuilt itself...and become a tribute to Jewish ingenuity."

The irony could not be more blatant; a ritual that for over two millennia united Jews in nations all over the world by linking them to the Holy Land should now be abandoned in the name of the latest political and cultural orthodoxy? Meanwhile, Sukkot speaks to a nation that has rebuilt itself, created a state, turned a desert into an Eden, and become a tribute to Jewish ingenuity – achievements

Methuselah as a seedling

that, Sukkot reminds us, are themselves a sign of God's beneficence and our chosenness.

Witness to this truth is borne by one of the central symbols of Sukkot. While date palms, as we have seen, were indeed reintroduced into the land of Israel, the uniquely Judean date palms, which towered over Israel at the time of the Roman invasion, had apparently disappeared forever. But in the 1960s the archeological excavators of the ancient fortress of Masada near the Dead Sea discovered a store of seeds from dates that had been stockpiled by the besieged defenders of the fortress against the advancing Roman legions.

At first regarded as uninteresting artifacts, the seeds lay neglected in a drawer until they were given to a scientist at the Arava Institute on a kibbutz in the Arava valley north of Eilat. There, after pre-treatment in a hormone-rich solution, they were planted by the botanist Elaine Solowey. The result? Here is the report of a journalist who visited Kibbutz Keturah a few months later:

> It has five leaves, stands fourteen inches high, and is nicknamed Methuselah. It looks like an ordinary date palm seedling, but for UCLA- educated botanist Elaine Solowey, it is a piece of history brought back to life.

> Planted on January 25, 2005, the seedling growing in the black pot in Solowey's nursery on this kibbutz in Israel's Arava desert is two thousand years old – more than twice as old as the nine-hundred-year-old biblical character who lent his name to the young tree. It is the oldest seed ever known to produce a viable young tree.... Scientists hope that the unique seedling will eventually yield vital clues to the medicinal properties of the fruit of the Judean date tree, which was long thought to be extinct.
>
> Until now.[13]

Today you can visit the tree. It is a flourishing, ten-foot-tall symbol of an eternal people and a resurrected nation. Planted in the sacred soil of the land of Israel, a date pit belonging to the dead defenders of Masada has grown into a date palm, a *lulav* tree, in the Jewish state.

Methuselah in full growth

Marking that state's fiftieth birthday in 2008, Paul Johnson wrote: "In the past half-century, more than one hundred new independent states have come into existence. Israel is the only one whose creation can be fairly called a miracle."[14] If that assertion is true, and it is certainly true, irrefutable testimony to the miracle is borne by this tree, at once unimaginably old and unimaginably new.

And there is more. Although, being male, Methuselah could produce no fruit on its own, a female tree, Hannah, germinated and grown by the same method, was successfully pollinated by Methuselah and by the mid-to-late teens of our present century was producing dates with, in Dr. Solowey's words, "a honey or caramel aftertaste." One can only imagine how glorious it would be in the fullness of time, what a joining of the generations, to be able to utilize a *lulav* from these first Judean date palms in millennia.

Yet, rightly understood, *every* observance of Sukkot involves just such a joining of the generations. To sit in a sukkah, to grasp a *lulav* and *etrog*, is to take one's place within the saga of the eternal people that defeated death, and to link oneself as a Jew to all that has been, all that is, and all that is yet to be.

Chapter Four
Hanukkah

▲ Enclosed outdoor menorahs in Jerusalem

The Hanukkah menorah and its ritual lighting are something special for Jews: symbols of identity and continuity, links to a people and a land. For many American Jews, indeed, kindling the candles on this holiday may form the most resonant Jewish symbol of all. But it was not always thus.

There are actually two historical stages to Hanukkah: first, the holiday as it existed while the Temple still stood, and second, the holiday that developed over two thousand years of Diaspora existence and persecution. A familiarity with both is critical for understanding Hanukkah in the age in which we now live, when most of the world's Jews live in freedom either in America or in the restored Jewish State of Israel.

The original Hanukkah story takes place in the first half of the second century BCE. At this point in time, the portion of Alexander the Great's empire that included Judea was ruled by the Hellenistic-Syrian dynasty of the Seleucid kings. In the year 175 BCE, King

Antiochus III was succeeded by his son Antiochus IV, known as Antiochus Epiphanes ("the illustrious").

A passionate apostle of Hellenistic culture, the new king was enthusiastically welcomed by many Judean Jews who were of a similar disposition. One of them, a priest of the Temple named Yeshua, adopted the Greek name Jason and bribed Antiochus to install him as the high priest, the *kohen gadol,* in place of his older brother. The deed done, Jason proceeded to incorporate Greek culture into Jerusalem, building at the very foot of the Temple Mount a gymnasium ostentatiously intended to serve as a center for Jews embracing Greek ways and the pagan worldview.

Our main source for these events is the book known as First Maccabees, a Jewish work from the period of the Second Temple that was composed originally in Hebrew but today exists only in translation. Here's how it recounts the story:

> In those days lawless men came forth from Israel and misled many, saying, "Let us go and make a covenant with the Gentiles round about us, for since we separated from them many evils have come upon us." This proposal pleased them, and some of the people eagerly went to the king. He authorized them to observe the ordinances of the Gentiles. So they built a gymnasium in Jerusalem, according to Gentile custom, and removed the marks of circumcision, and abandoned the holy covenant. (I Macc. 1:11–15)

Jason's gymnasium in Jerusalem, with its celebration of the athletic human form, was thus a physical embodiment of the intrusion of paganism into Judea. As for Jason himself, some local enthusiasts of Greek culture found him to be not pagan *enough*. Soon another Jew, by the name of Menelaus – possibly not descended from a priestly family at all – convinced Antiochus to install *him* as the high priest instead of Jason.

And so the fight was on. When Antiochus was rumored to have died in battle in Egypt, Jason mustered forces to overthrow Menelaus, but the king, very much alive, sent his general Apollonius to reinstall Menelaus and to make the pagan way of life legally mandatory. The result, according to First Maccabees:

> Many even from Israel gladly adopted [the king's] religion; they sacrificed to idols and profaned the Sabbath. And the king sent letters by messengers to Jerusalem and the cities of Judah; he directed them to follow customs strange to the land, to forbid burnt offerings, sacrifices, and drink offerings in the sanctuary, to profane Sabbaths and feasts, to defile the sanctuary and the priests, to build altars and sacred precincts and shrines for idols, to sacrifice swine and unclean animals, and to leave their sons uncircumcised. (I Macc. 1:43–48)

This campaign did not go unopposed. The Temple altar was first utilized for idolatrous worship on the twenty-fifth day of the Hebrew month of Kislev. At about the same time, a rebellion broke out in the town of Modi'in outside Jerusalem, led by a priestly patriarch named Mattathias whose family bore the name *Ḥashmonai*, Hasmonean.

Who, then, were the Maccabees? This calls for a brief digression. Although the origin of the name "Hasmonean" is unclear, one fact is certain: Mattathias's band of men were never called Maccabees; there were no Maccabees. But one of Mattathias's many sons, Judah, was known as *Makabee*, a nickname probably originating from the Aramaic word for hammer and referring to Judah's proficiency as a warrior. The plural, Maccabees, as in the Jewish book of First Maccabees, became

"Judah was known as *Makabee,* a nickname probably originating from the Aramaic word for hammer and referring to Judah's proficiency as a warrior."

attached to the family only when that book and its companion volume, Second Maccabees, were canonized as part of the Christian Bible. In modern parlance we call them Maccabees, but they were Hasmoneans.

Moreover, the war commenced by the Hasmoneans was not really between Jews and non-Jews; it was a civil war between traditional Jews and the Jewish Hellenizers (in Hebrew, *mityavnim*), with the latter backed by the military might of the Seleucids.

The patriarch Mattathias briefly led the rebellion, but when he died the leadership passed to his son Judah "the hammer." About two years after the first pagan sacrifice in Jerusalem, Judah led an assault on the occupied sacred city. His stirring words, reported in the third chapter of First Maccabees, would languish largely in obscurity until resurrected by Winston Churchill who, in his first radio broadcast as British prime minister, in the midst of his country's darkest hour, invoked the story of Hanukkah and Judah's words:

> Arm yourselves, and be ye valiant men, and see that ye be in readiness against the morning, that ye may fight with these nations that are assembled together against us to destroy us and our sanctuary. For it is better for us to die in battle than to behold the calamities of our people and our sanctuary.... As the will of God is in heaven, so let Him do. (I Maccabees 3:58–60)

In the event, Judah's forces succeeded in conquering the Temple even as much of Jerusalem remained held by the enemy. Proceeding to purify the sanctuary, they immediately encountered an unresolvable question of Jewish ritual: what to do with the altar.

A pagan altar in the Temple should obviously be destroyed, but this altar had been built by the prophet Ezra when the Second Temple was first constructed in the sixth century BCE. How could they keep it? But how could they not? They decided not to destroy it, but to move the pieces to a safe place. A new altar was built, and it was finished on the second anniversary of the twenty-fifth of Kislev. Judah's men then celebrated a *ḥanukkah*, a dedication – that is, of

Magdala stone

the new altar – and instituted the observance of eight days of commemorative rejoicing every year.

At this juncture in history, there was no kindling of candles in every Jewish home. The eight days were celebrated with psalms of thanksgiving to God, as a passage in the Jewish liturgy recounts: *Vekavu shemonat yemei ḥanukkah eilu lehodot ulehallel leshimkha hagadol* – "They ordained these eight days of Hanukkah to give thanks and praise to Thy great name."

Why eight days? The answer lies in the only *biblical* holiday that lasts eight days: the seven days of Sukkot followed immediately by Shemini Atzeret, the "Eighth Day of Assembly." Thus, a separate

Jewish account of the Hanukkah story, known as Second Maccabees, offers the following:

> It happened that on the same day on which the sanctuary had been profaned by the foreigners, the purification of the sanctuary took place, that is, on the 25th day of the same month, which was Kislev. And they celebrated it for eight days with rejoicing, in the manner of the Festival of Booths, remembering how not long before, during the Festival of Booths, they had been wandering in the mountains and caves like wild animals.... They offered hymns of thanksgiving to Him who had given success to the purifying of His own holy place. They decreed by public ordinance and vote that the whole nation of the Jews should observe these days every year. (II Macc. 10:5–8)

Hanukkah was thus originally conceived as a Sukkot in December, ostensibly as a means of making up for the holiday that the Hasmoneans had most recently missed. But there is a deeper meaning to this link between the two holidays. As we saw in our previous chapter, Sukkot was observed in the Temple, around the altar, with the pilgrims waving the symbols of nature and agriculture in worship of God the Creator as a response to, and in rejection of, the pagan divinization of nature itself. In this light, marking an eight-day celebration of Hanukkah was the Hasmonean way of expressing

> "A commemoration of the triumph of monotheism over paganism, Hanukkah represents nothing less than one of the tipping points in the history of the world."

and celebrating the fact that now there was one small patch of land on a mountaintop in Jerusalem that the pagan world had not swallowed up – a fact that would be remembered for eight days every year, with psalms and praise.

In this sense, Hanukkah was first and foremost a commemoration of the triumph of monotheism over paganism. And, as such, it represented nothing less than one of the tipping points in the history of the world. For in 164 BCE, monotheism was known only in Judea. Had the Hasmoneans not succeeded at this crucial moment, there would have been no monotheism at all.

This very point was made by the late Christopher Hitchens, an influential British writer and an avowed *enemy* of biblical religion. In an essay titled "Bah, Hanukkah," composed in the same hot distemper that marks most of his writings about faith, Hitchens acknowledged that monotheism had survived thanks only to Judah and his troops – but this, he asserted, had been disastrous, and

> not just for the Jews.... When the fanatics of Palestine won that victory, and when Judaism repudiated Athens for Jerusalem, the development of the whole of humanity was terribly retarded.

Therefore, argued Hitchens, to celebrate Hanukkah

> is to celebrate not just the triumph of tribal Jewish backwardness but also the accidental birth of Judaism's bastard child in the shape of Christianity. You might think that masochism could do no more. Except that it always can. Without the precedents of Orthodox Judaism and Roman Christianity... there would be no Islam, either.[1]

Hitchens had a point: Without Hanukkah, there would have been only a pagan world, devoid of monotheism. But this is precisely why we do celebrate. For anyone who believes that civilization needs not only Athens but also Jerusalem, and that from the Jewish moral vision the world received ideas unknown to Athens – ideas like the sacred inviolability of every human life, stemming from creation in the image of God; sexual morality; the centrality of marriage and the family; and the purposiveness of history – for anyone who believes these ideas are essential, Hitchens's bitter hatred of Hanukkah only underlines the reason why this festival is so significant, and (to use his phrase) "not just for the Jews."

The great American statesman John Adams – whose thoughts on the Jewish contribution to civilization we quoted in the Introduction – may never have celebrated Hanukkah, but he could have had Hitchens and his ilk in mind when, referring to those who hate Judaism, he wrote:

> Let the wits joke; [let] the philosopher sneer. What then? It has pleased the Provident of the first cause that Abraham should give religion, not only to Hebrews but to Christians and Mahometans, the greatest part of the modern civilized world.[2]

This, then, was Hanukkah from the moment that Judah captured the Temple. But two centuries later, in 70 CE, the Temple was destroyed, in large part because of the failings of the Hasmonean family itself, whose infighting facilitated the Romans' determination to gain a foothold in, and ultimately sovereignty over, Judea.

The question, then, was obvious: What would happen to Hanukkah now? How could a holiday centered on the restoration of monotheism in the Temple continue in existence when the Roman pagans had succeeded in destroying the Temple and reducing it to ruins?

To that question, the rabbinic sages had an answer. They formulated it by focusing on a miracle that had occurred during the Hasmoneans' cleansing of the Temple two centuries earlier. The miracle: A small flask of oil that ought to have fueled a flame for only a single day proved sufficient to keep the Menorah, the Temple candelabrum, burning for no fewer than eight days in all. Now, the rabbis said, we may not be able to celebrate for eight days at the altar of monotheism in the Temple, but we can celebrate, and reenact, that eight-day miracle.

This rabbinic institution is mocked by many today. Who creates holidays around so minor a miracle? Hitchens, for one, is aghast:

> As a consequence of the successful Maccabean revolt against Hellenism, so it is said, a puddle of olive oil that should have lasted only for one day managed to burn for eight days. Wow! Certain proof, not just of an Almighty, but of an Almighty with a special fondness for fundamentalists.[3]

One hesitates to take such bigoted language seriously. But first of all, Hanukkah, as the name of the holiday suggests, was not originally instituted to mark only that miracle, nor, secondly, did the rabbis fail to recognize that the victory over the Greek forces and their pagan Jewish allies was a miracle greater than the endurance of a flask of oil. If, after the destruction of the Temple, the rabbis chose to commemorate that one small supernatural occurrence, it was because of the powerful metaphor it represented: If a small flask could endure for an unnaturally long time, then so could the Jewish people. If the flames of the Temple Menorah could burn beyond expectation, then, even with Jerusalem destroyed, the beacon that was Judaism could survive.

The Kindling of the Hanukkah Lights, Moritz Daniel Oppenheim

Hence the obligation to light flames in every Jewish home in remembrance of the Menorah miracle. And note the word "home": the obligation was formulated in the Talmud (Shabbat 21b) as *ner ish u'veito*, a "lamp for every man and his household." Remarkably, the obligation was to light not in the synagogue, a tradition that only came into being a thousand years later, but in the home. By this the sages meant to communicate that the Jewish *family* was the means through which the Jews would outlast their enemies, the means through which the small flask that was a tiny people would burn brightly and outlive all others.

In examining the details of this obligation, something interesting emerges. The original command was to place the menorah at the entrance to the house on the outside (*al petaḥ beito mi'baḥutz*), thereby adorning the entryway not only by means of the mezuzah with its parchment on the right side but also with the Hanukkah lights on the left. By design, both would be seen by passersby as marking the presence of a Jewish home.

In time, over the centuries of persecution, the menorah was brought indoors. But Jews still lit it in an internal doorway opposite the mezuzah. Only in modernity did we begin lighting in a window where the menorah could be seen by the public.

In Jerusalem today, and in some traditionalist homes elsewhere, the menorah is once again lit in the outer doorway, thus bringing

Arch of Titus: Menorah

Arch of Titus: Titus in triumph

together these two sublime symbols of our faith: on the right, the scroll of the mezuzah on which is inscribed the most famous expression of monotheistic faith – "Hear O Israel, the Lord our God, the Lord is one" – and on the left, the lamp of Hanukkah, the reification of Judaism's endurance.

The entry to a Jewish home as it appeared on Hanukkah can be contrasted to another entryway adorned by a menorah.

That other portal is the Arch of Titus, a classic example of the *arcus triumphalis*: a monumental structure, invented by the Romans, through which a triumphant general would pass on his return to the imperial capital. Titus's arch, built to celebrate the Roman conquest of Jerusalem, depicts on its frieze the returning procession of the Temple's marauders. Among the vessels hoisted aloft by the victorious soldiers is, most famously, the great golden Menorah.

And that is not all. The purloined Temple Menorah on one side of the arch declares that the special relationship of the Jews with their God is over and done with. Meanwhile, the frieze on the opposite side depicts a scene no less loaded with significance for the Romans of the day. Giving us the triumphant entrance into the city of Titus himself, accompanied by the winged goddess of victory, it marks the divinization of the emperor and the triumph of paganism.

Today, then, are we not surely entitled to understand the method of Jewish lighting on Hanukkah as a direct theological *response* to the arch and all it signifies? Against the arch's pagan gods on one side and the captured unlit Menorah on the other, Jewish doorways had the mezuzah of monotheism on one side and the lit menorah of Judaism on the other. Contra the arch, these two images proclaimed that so long as the Jewish family and home continued to exist, monotheism would endure, Judaism would endure, the memory of Jerusalem would endure, and remembrance of the Temple would endure. Even stripped of sovereignty, scattered around the globe, made into objects of hatred, Jews would create homes – miniature temples, spiritual sanctuaries – whose very entryways signaled that here was a haven of divine benevolence.

Over the centuries, the construction of triumphal arches continued. We know of many more made in Rome itself; still later models would include Napoleon's Arc de Triomphe in Paris and the Marble Arch in London. All are expressions of empire, manifestations of military might. But while every one of those empires ended up on the ash heap of history, the Jewish people remained, adorning the entrance to their homes with mezuzah and menorah, longing for their land and for a return to political sovereignty while knowing that their ultimate eternity lay in *ner ish u'veito*: a lamp for every Jewish home.

One does not have to be Jewish to be struck by the comparison. In 1853, Ferdinand Gregorovius, a German historian of Rome, described how, wandering one day into the city's Jewish ghetto, he noticed that the menorah, carved on walls and painted in the synagogue, had remained a vital symbol of Judaism. Having visited the Arch of Titus with its proclamation of Judaism's death, he beheld with wonder the abundant evidence of living Judaism:

> If we descend from the Arch of Titus toward the Tiber and wander through the ghetto, we notice the seven-branched candelabrum engraved here and there on the walls of the inhabited houses. It is the same design which we just now saw on the Arch, but here it is alive as the functioning symbol of the Jewish religion, and to this day there dwell in these houses descendants of

> the Jews whom Titus once led [into exile] in triumph. If we visit the synagogue of the Hebrews, we see the same sculptures of the Ark of the Covenant, the golden table, the jubilee trumpet, decorating its walls.
>
> Beneath the figures of the Temple vessels which Titus once brought to Rome, the Jewish people, still persisting, still undestroyed, offers up its prayers to the ancient Jehovah of Jerusalem. Jehovah has proved more powerful than the Capitoline Jupiter.[4]

Gregorovius was right to be awestruck. And an even more wondrous response to the arch was yet to come. Among the remaining Roman Jewish community, forced for centuries into a ghetto and obliged to take an oath of loyalty to the pope, it had become an established custom to refrain from walking under the Arch of Titus. With the birth of Israel, the Jews in Rome, in a famous photograph, gathered at the arch to walk in the opposite direction from that trodden by Titus's troops – thereby symbolizing the reversal of what the arch proclaimed.

Nor is this the only reversal witnessed by history; far from it. Imagine the amazement of Titus, or Vespasian, or later, Constantine, had any of them been told that in two thousand years' time nothing would remain of the Roman Empire and relatively little even of the once-universal Latin language. Imagine their amazement upon being further informed that, simultaneously, Jews had reestablished sovereignty over their land, reversed the effects of the Roman conquest, and created a flourishing society speaking the language of their ancestors.

The flask of oil in the Menorah burns still. Today, Jews may not have the Temple, but they do have Jerusalem. Although the messianic era is not yet here, the Jewish people have built a state in Judea more powerful than any ever held by the Hasmoneans. In our time, too, both the Hanukkah of the Second Temple and the Hanukkah of the exile speak to us profoundly and with sharp contemporary relevance.

For, sadly, while few today worship Zeus or Athena, the values of the pagan world are once again celebrated. Nature is again divinized, traditional sexual mores are dismissed as outmoded, and the infinite innate value of every human life is far from taken for granted. The original, civilization-saving Hanukkah is as needed today as it ever was, as are its faithful Jewish celebrants. As the great American writer Mark Twain once observed:

> The Jew has made a marvelous fight in this world, in all the ages; and has done it with his hands tied behind him. All things are mortal but the Jew; all other forces pass, but he remains. What is the secret of his immortality?[5]

The "secret," once again, is *ner ish u'veito,* a lamp for every Jewish household. Judaism is transmitted first and foremost not through military might or political power but through the home: the Jewish fortress throughout the centuries, an edifice so seemingly insignificant, but ultimately so extraordinary, that no empire could overcome it.

Chapter Five
Tu BiShvat

The first Israeli film to achieve international acclaim was *Sallah Shabati* (1964). A biting comedy, it skewered the manners and mores of the socialist Ashkenazi elite that was then in sole charge of much of Israeli life. Starring the actor Topol (later of *Fiddler on the Roof* fame), the film follows the adventures, misadventures, and frustrations of a Mizraḥi (that is, a Middle Eastern or North African Jew) who immigrates to Israel in its early years. At every turn, Sallah Shabati encounters injustices, hardships, and frustrations, to which he responds with often hilarious ingenuity and the stubborn remnants of his pride. His very name, summarizing the pathos of his experience, is a pun on the Hebrew phrase *Sliḥah shebati*, "Sorry I came."

Stationed on a kibbutz, Shabati is put to work planting saplings: the first stage of a future forest. Though the film does not specify the time of year, we can deduce that it is around Tu BiShvat, the fifteenth day of the Jewish month of Shevat, a day known as *Rosh HaShanah LaIlanot*, the New Year (or Festival) for Trees, and a time when donors to the state's forestation project arrive annually to behold what their financial contributions have made possible.

On the kibbutz, just before a group of American Jews pulls up in their chauffeured sedan, the bureaucrat in charge installs a bold sign: "Here Will Rise the Jacob Birnbaum Forest." Mr. Birnbaum arrives, has his picture taken, and departs. Rushing about, the bureaucrat uproots the sign and replaces it with another: "Here Will Rise the Pearl Sonnenstein Forest."

"Why all this rigamarole?" Shabati inquires. The bureaucrat responds that "every one of these American Jews wants his own forest." "But it's dishonest," Shabati protests. And thus, Mrs. Sonnenstein, as she alights, discovers Sallah uprooting the just-planted saplings. "What are you doing?!" the bureaucrat yells. Shabati replies: "This is Birnbaum's forest! Sonnenstein needs her own!" He is of course fired on the spot.

For present-day viewers, the film captures a moment in the saga of modern Israel that highlights the land's transformation over the past seventy-five years from a hardscrabble third-world country reliant on American Jewish philanthropy to an agricultural and technological powerhouse. But this particular scene also serves as a metaphor for Tu BiShvat itself – a holiday that defines Jews today by their ties to the past and to a nation as well as by their link to a land and their obligations to its future.

Or does it? Unfortunately, for many Jews today, Tu BiShvat has become an occasion to celebrate causes and projects wholly unconnected with Jewish identity, unrooted in the Jewish past, and unmoored from the values that Judaism holds dear.

Let's go back in time in order to move forward.

For much of Jewish history, Tu BiShvat was actually not a holiday at all. In the Talmud, the day represents nothing more than one in a series of legal deadlines, in this case regarding the obligation to offer tithed portions of the year's crops to the Levites in the Temple. For fruits in particular, the end of one fiscal year and the beginning of the next was marked by Tu BiShvat, the date chosen by the rabbinical academy of Hillel as the point in very early spring when fruit trees began to flower. Thus, a farmer in the land of Israel would take (i.e., tithe) 10 percent of every crop that had flowered between the fifteenth of Shevat of one year and the next.

For centuries, this is all that Tu BiShvat was: a Jewish legal version of what December 31 (the cutoff date for calculating the previous year's taxes) represents for many Americans today. How, then, did an instance of the Talmud's legal regime become a sacred festival?

The laws of tithing, according to the Talmud, apply only to produce grown in the Holy Land; they are therefore known in Jewish law as biblical commandments that reflect the sanctity of the land and the fruits nurtured by its soil. Thus, for Jews outside the land, marking Tu BiShvat became a long-distance means of connecting to the land itself and celebrating the botanical specimens that figure in the Bible.

Our marking of the holiday, like many of our traditions today, traces back to the mystical circle of Safed (Tzfat) in northern Israel. The sixteenth-century kabbalists of that city composed a liturgy and created a series of rituals for the day, prominently featuring what became known as a Tu BiShvat seder. The ceremonies paralleled the Passover Seder but with the unleavened bread replaced by produce and with the four cups of wine progressing from lighter (that is,

View of Safed

▲
Carob fruit

white) to darker (deep red) vintages, symbolizing the four seasons from winter through spring and from summer to autumn.

Reconnecting with the land in this fashion was a relatively easy step for Sephardim living along the Mediterranean littoral, whose celebrations centered on the seven species of fruit for which the land of Israel was biblically known, among them grapes, figs, pomegranates, olives, and dates. It was much less easy for Ashkenazi Jews experiencing Tu BiShvat in the frigid winters of Eastern Europe, who would eat any fruit they could get their hands on that had once grown from a tree rooted in that sacred soil.

That is why, for Orthodox Jews of many generations, including my own, Tu BiShvat became concretized in the eating of one fruit in particular: the carob, whose name derives from the Hebrew *ḥaruv* and whose Yiddish name, *bokser*, is short for the German *bokshornbaum* (that is, the tree with ram's-horn-shaped fruit).

There is no question that *bokser* had long been native to the Holy Land; ancient carob seeds dating to the Neolithic period have been found in archeological digs. Yet while the Bible celebrates the seven species, and rabbinic Judaism (as we saw in the chapter on Sukkot) elevates the perfections of the *etrog*, nary a mention in the Bible is made of the *ḥaruv*, though it was undoubtedly a fruit in which the Holy Land abounded.

The reason for the silence is self-evident: In the dried version that generations of Jews experienced it, and as accurately described by the language columnist known as Philologos, the fruit was both "hard as nails to bite into" and yielding, "if you [hadn't] meanwhile broken all your teeth, a mealy substance that has been described as smelling like limburger cheese." As if to confirm such modern judgments, the Talmud itself states several times that carob is *maakhhal beheimah*, food fit (only) for beasts.

If Ashkenazi Jews nevertheless ate carob on Tu BiShvat, it was because they had no other way of connecting to the land they loved. As Gil Marks notes in his *Encyclopedia of Jewish Food*:

> In the days before quick transport and refrigeration, the carob's hard, dry texture made it one of the few fruits grown in the land of Israel capable of withstanding long-distance shipping without spoilage, and therefore was available to Ashkenazim.[1]

Indeed, many Jews in Eastern Europe and North America did more than tolerate *bokser*. Rabbi Berel Wein, who grew up and celebrated Tu BiShvat in the veritably Arctic winters of Chicago, recalls that

> although the *bokser* was hard as a rock and tasteless as wood, ... I noticed that my parents, Jews of an earlier generation who were born before there was a state of Israel, ... ate their pieces slowly and with great affection. Only later in my life did I realize that eating that

> piece of *bokser* validated their hope and belief that the land of Israel would yet flourish and grow under Jewish sovereignty, and that the vineyards and orchards of the land promised to us by our prophets would become abundant reality.[2]

Tu BiShvat, then, reflected for Jews the *rootedness* of Jewish national identity. We moderns often like to say, or pretend, that our identity is not predetermined but malleable, that it can be shed and replaced like a suit of clothes, that we can be whoever we wish to be. And to a certain extent, that is true. Judaism insists, however, that such an attitude, taken to an extreme, denies human nature – or what we might call the tree-like nature of human existence.

Let me explain. In forbidding the wanton destruction of fruit trees, Deuteronomy introduces an interesting analogy: *Ki haadam eitz hasadeh*, "For man is akin to a tree in the field." To Rabbi Soloveitchik, this seemingly strange comparison suggests precisely that man, much like a tree, is in fact integrally connected with his (human) roots, and even largely defined by them. And here another aspect of *bokser* reveals itself. The carob, says the Talmud, has longer roots than most other Israelite trees; to eat its fruit was thus, for Jews in the Diaspora, to link themselves with an identity impervious to the often inimical forces of their surrounding environment.

> "Sitting at their Tu BiShvat seder – the mystics of Safed prayed for the time when Jewish life in the Holy Land would bloom and blossom, flower and flourish."

In this respect, the hopes and dreams of the kabbalistic creators of Tu BiShvat celebrations have been vindicated. For imagine a community of these Jewish mystics at a Tu BiShvat seder in northern Israel, at a time of year when the trees were still shorn of leaves, the wind was fierce, and the mountains that lay only a bit farther north were capped with snow. The season would thus in some measure have paralleled what was then the winter of Jewish history – over much of the land of Israel itself, the earth lay frigid and barren, the orchards were empty, and the cities, including Jerusalem, held few Jews.

And so they sat at their Seder and pondered the fact that underneath the whiteness of winter, deep within the ground, the rain was gathering, that above the ground the trees were beginning to bud, and that spring was preparing to arrive. So, too, they would allow themselves to hope. The Jewish love for and loyalty to the land of Israel were laying the groundwork for an age when the bitterness would end, the spring of Jewish history would arrive, and once again Jews would lovingly work the land and observe the Torah's agricultural strictures, including the tithing of fruit, and the prophet Isaiah's exclamation would finally be fulfilled: "For God has consoled Zion, and transformed its deserts into a garden of God" (51:3).

Sitting at this Tu Bishvat seder, proceeding from white wine to deepening shades of red, the mystics of Safed prayed for the time when Jewish life in the Holy Land would bloom and blossom, flower and flourish, when the fields would be full with wheat, the orchards with *etrogim* and oranges, and when even the deserts, defying expectations, would be transposed into Edens, culminating in an extraordinary autumn and in the celebration of Sukkot when Jews from all over the world would converge on Jerusalem to celebrate the harvest of the land.

Today, however, for much of world Jewry, Tu BiShvat, rather than embodying a link to a land and a people, has morphed into a "Jewish" version of Earth Day. In some of its most egregious manifestations, the holiday, as Tevi Troy writes, has been dragged into service by Jews and Jewish groups to advance "the importance of eating locally grown foods, reducing one's carbon footprint, opposing fracking, and exploring why Jews should become vegans (or at the very least vegetarians)." Most American synagogues of all denominations, Troy adds, "have seized on [this holiday] as an opportunity for communal service to the environment."[3]

It is of course true, Troy notes, that "Judaism was and remains an environmentally friendly religion." But its view of the environment "is based in the sense of responsible individual stewardship and in the fundamental goodness of Creation rather than in a critique of humankind"[4] as a preternaturally wasteful and debased enemy of the environment.

The point according to Troy is "not that individual environmental programs are necessarily bad or problematic in and of themselves,"[5] or that Jews wishing to help the environment should refrain from doing their civic part. The question, rather, is whether a Jewish observance whose authentically Jewish purpose dates back millennia should be simply grafted on as an appendage to a movement with its own divergent values, purposes, and rationales, some of them in tension with – if not overtly antagonistic to – Judaism.

Again and again, Troy concludes, "Judaism has outlived many an ancient civilization by aiming to follow the ways of the Torah." By contrast, "a Judaism that tethers itself to the culture around it and worships the idols of the day detaches itself from its own deepest convictions."[6] Regrettably, even the website of the Jewish National Fund (JNF), an organization that has mobilized Jews all over the world to donate funds for planting trees *in Israel*, proudly asserted that the Jewish festival of trees bespeaks "the dedication to ecology, environmentalism, and conservation that JNF has always championed".[7]

With due respect to the importance of conservation, the fact is that Tu BiShvat has never had anything to do either with conservation or "ecology [and] environmentalism" *per se*. Of course, you might say that these modern movements are still, in some amorphous sense, about trees. But their Jewish followers and supporters are oblivious of the Bible's teaching that we Jews, like so many trees in the field, flourish first and foremost when we recognize our own roots and what we owe to the land that has spiritually sustained us throughout our existence as a people. In that light, the story of Tu BiShvat reflects two miracles: the miracle of a millennial Jewish existence buttressed by loyalty to and love for the Holy Land, and the miracle that is Israeli agriculture today – at once a vindication of that loyal love and a fulfillment of biblical prophecy in our time.

In foreseeing an eventual destruction of the Israelite polity by its enemies, the Torah warns that, with Israel exiled from the land, the soil itself will remain barren (Lev. 26:33). And indeed, although empire after empire, from Rome to Byzantium, from the Christian West to the Muslim East, invested blood, toil, and treasure into cultivating the land of Israel, what emerged from the land in return was aridity. Visiting the region as late as the mid-nineteenth century, Mark Twain described what he saw:

> The hills are barren, they are dull of color, they are unpicturesque in shape. The valleys are unsightly deserts tinged with a feeble vegetation that has an expression about it of being sorrowful and despondent. The Dead Sea and the Sea of Galilee sleep in the midst of a vast stretch of hill and plain wherein the eye rests upon no pleasant tint, no striking object, no soft picture dreaming in a purple haze or mottled with the shadows of the clouds. Every outline is harsh, every feature is distinct, there is no perspective – distance works no enchantment here. It is a hopeless, dreary, heartbroken land.[8]

So it was – but no longer. On February 14, 1949 – the fifteenth day of the month of Shevat – the Knesset, the parliament of the State of Israel, convened for the first time. On his way to the assembly in Jerusalem, David Ben-Gurion paused on the road at Shaar Hagai, also known as Bab el-Wad. There, just one year earlier, hundreds of Jewish soldiers had died in the attempt to break the Arab siege of Jerusalem. And there, as captured in a famous photograph, Ben-Gurion planted a tree. That image marks not only the miraculous restoration of Jewish sovereignty but also the miraculous rebirth of the land's fertility.

Ben-Gurion planting a tree on Tu BiShvat, Shaar Hagai 1949

Look at what has occurred: Isaiah's prophetic verses have come true in our time, and God has indeed consoled Zion, transformed its desert into an Eden, its wilderness into a garden. With an appreciation of this miracle must come a reverence for the love and faith of generations past, and an obligation to pass on that same love and faith to our posterity.

Never has there been more meaning in the Jewish festival of the Holy Land's trees – whole forests of which were the work of the fictional Sallah Shabati and legions of his real-life fellow Jews from every corner of the earth. But at the same time, never has this festival been more misunderstood and misused. We Jews owe those who came before us a Tu BiShvat worthy of their faith, and of our future.

Beit Shemesh then and now

Chapter Six
Purim

In the early 1950s, an increasingly paranoid Joseph Stalin turned his attention once again to the Jews: the targets of paranoid tyrants always and everywhere. A plan was even put into motion for their deportation from the USSR by the hundreds of thousands. Then, suddenly, on March 1, 1953, he suffered a stroke and died several days later.

On that same March 1, as the famed Soviet refusenik Natan Sharansky would later recall,

> I came home from kindergarten and my father explained to me that Stalin was a monster, killed a lot of people, that we Jews were next in line, that he was going to send us to Siberia, but that now he was dead and we were saved, and that I should remember all my life that miracles happened, but I should not tell it to anybody; I should do what everybody does. And the next morning I am going to kindergarten, I am crying with all the children over the death of Stalin, I am singing songs how grateful we are to Stalin, and I remember that miracles happened, I should be happy. Happy, in other words, that Stalin was dead. (*Fear No Evil*, 1988)

Decorated megillah, Italy 1616

March 1, 1953 was also, according to the Jewish calendar, the holiday of Purim. A coincidence? The downfall of the wicked, the seemingly providential salvation of the Jewish people – such events can be acknowledged by Jews even in a world where most do not recognize the existence of the Hebrew God. Indeed, this same lesson is understood by many to be the central point of the biblical book of Esther, the scriptural source of our Purim celebrations.

The book of Esther, known colloquially by Jews as the Megillah (literally, "the scroll"), is unlike any other book in the Bible. It contains no prophecies, no revelations, no celestial visions. Never – not once – does the name of God actually appear. Moreover, the tale told by the book takes place not in the land of Israel but in the most pagan setting: Shushan, the capital of Persia. The time is some point in the early to mid-fifth century BCE; although the text does refer briefly to the Babylonians' prior destruction of Jerusalem in 586 BCE, no allusion is made to the Temple, the dwelling place of the Divine.

Let's briefly summarize the story. Xerxes, or as he is known in the book, Ahasuerus (in Hebrew, *Aḥashveirosh*), king of Persia, is overcome by drunken rage and decides to rid himself of his wife. In a contest eerily akin to a reality TV show, he conducts a search for a new queen. His affections fall on a beautiful woman named Esther, who, unbeknownst to him, is from a Jewish family. Esther has been ordered by her cousin Mordecai, himself a minor official of the royal court, not to disclose her identity.

Haman, the vizier of Persia, driven by hatred of Mordecai, convinces the king to issue a decree ordering the genocide of the empire's Jews. Mordecai then urges Esther to reveal her identity to the king and to plead for her people. Originally hesitant, but urged by her cousin into action, Esther carries out a politically brilliant strategy of her own devising. Playing on the king's paranoia, she deflects his native rage onto Haman, who is ultimately hanged on the same gallows he has prepared for Mordecai. Now, with the king's blessing and encouragement, Jews across the empire gather to wage a counteroffensive battle against Haman's anti-Semitic allies, and the Jews emerge victorious.

The Triumph of Mordecai, Rembrandt van Rijn

This is the story recalled every year on the holiday of Purim. The point of the story has to do first and foremost with the lesson taught by Natan Sharansky's father: never lose the ability to see God, and to discern the miraculous, even in the midst of an evil and godless empire.

As Rabbi Yoel Bin-Nun has noted, the inclusion of the book of Esther in the biblical canon serves to raise a fundamental question: in an upside-down world, who rules?

> Were the Megillah, the scroll of Esther, to have been omitted from [Scripture], we would have seen and recognized the presence of the Almighty only within circumstances where His Name may be legitimately uttered, within a reality where Jewish spirituality can legitimately be maintained. The book of Esther is thus indispensable, as it demonstrates God's presence even in places where His name may not be introduced, even in situations where one may not pray, study Torah, or be engaged in anything sacred. The Megillah shows us the reality of divine providence at work in the topsy-turvy world of the royal court in Shushan, where everything appears to happen… with no spiritual dimension whatsoever.[1]

As a theological point, this is beautifully put, and no doubt true. We Jews do believe in the reality of miracles, in the possibility of divine intervention, and in seeing providence where others do not. It is this way of looking at the world that the book of Esther encourages.

And yet, in my view, this does not quite get to the heart of the drama of the book and the central theme of the holiday. If Purim were primarily about providence, about discovering the divine in the midst of the vulgar and profane, we would devote our day of celebration to recognizing God's presence, to prayer and thanksgiving. We would certainly recite the biblical psalms of praise – the Hallel – that are part of the liturgy on every Jewish festival.

But Hallel is not recited on Purim (as the Talmud itself notes), and very few of the day's rituals and obligations focus on, or even make reference to, God. We are charged to read aloud the book of Esther, and then we spend the rest of the day feasting with our fellow Jews and ensuring, through gifts to other Jews, that we will have played a role in their feasts as well. Purim is marked, according to the book of Esther itself, as a time of "feasting and joy, exchanging delicacies with one another, and sending gifts to the poor."

No other ancient Jewish holiday entails anything like this. Rosh HaShanah's central ritual is the shofar, sounding both a clarion call from God and a Jewish cry to God; Yom Kippur's central duty is atonement before God; on Sukkot, we sit in a ramshackle hut as a reminder of God's protection; on Hanukkah we light candles to commemorate the defeat of the pagans by the one true God; at the Passover Seder we recreate our redemption at the hands of God; and on Shavuot we mark our gratitude for the gift of the Torah, the law of God. Purim, and only Purim, codifies (in rabbinic parlance) certain rites between one Jew and another rather than between a Jew and God.

"Even more than recognizing the presence of the divinity, the book of Esther is about the demands of Jewish loyalty."

This by itself should alert us to the fact that Purim tells us something not only about the divinity but also about ourselves, and that even more than recognizing the presence of the divinity, the book of Esther is about the demands of Jewish loyalty. This aspect of Purim has been often overlooked, yet no aspect speaks to us more profoundly today. Why is that and how so?

Addressing the rise and triumph of Western individualism, and the man-is-the-measure-of-all-things worldview associated with the age of the Enlightenment, Rabbi Jonathan Sacks notes that

> [s]everal centuries of Western thought have left us with the idea that when we choose how to live, we are on our own. Nothing in the past binds us. We are whoever we

> choose to be. We enter the world with a clean slate on which we can draw any self-portrait we wish.[2]

"So axiomatic" is this modern idea of individualism, writes Rabbi Sacks, that we are "all too unaware of the intellectual history that lies behind it." Helpfully, he traces some of the key figures and moments: "David Hume stating that we cannot derive 'ought' from 'is,' Immanuel Kant placing autonomy at the heart of moral life...Jean-Paul Sartre arguing that 'existence precedes essence.'"[3]

Against this whole complex of ideas, Rabbi Sacks continues, Jewish life presents a sustained counterstatement:

> To be a Jew is to know that this cannot be the full story of who I am. A melody is more than a sequence of disconnected notes. A painting is something other than a random set of brushstrokes. The past has meaning in terms of its place within the whole, so that if history has meaning, then the lives that make it up must in some way be joined to one another as characters in a narrative.[4]

The point is that Judaism, Jewish thought, begins with a profoundly unmodern, politically incorrect, and thoroughly countercultural idea: that as Jews we are not first and foremost individuals and that, whether we like it or not, we are part of a story, part of a family, part of a people – and that this is actually a central and unalterable aspect of ourselves.

With this in mind, we can take note of an important word that does not appear in most of the Bible but crops up countless times in Esther: the word *Yehudi*, or Jew. Throughout the Hebrew Bible we are largely called *Yisrael*, Israel, but in Esther, as in our parlance today, we are called *Yehudim*, Jews. The appellation derives from Yehudah (Judah), one of the twelve sons of the patriarch Jacob and the ancestor of one of the twelve tribes of ancient Israel.

There are, of course, historical reasons for the development of the term "Jew." During the period of the First Temple, the kingdom of Israel, united under David and Solomon, split into two. The southern monarchy, still ruled by the Davidic dynasty, became known by the name of Judah, its dominant tribe. (It also included the small tribe of Benjamin.) After the northern kingdom was wiped out by Assyria in 721 BCE, with its ten tribes carried away into captivity, the Israelites dwelling in the south became the sole bearers of the Abrahamic faith; they became known as *Yehudim*, "Judahites" or "Judeans," and their faith eventually became known as Judaism.

Many people known as *Yehudim* today do not descend from the southern kingdom of Judah. For example, all Levites, (of whom I myself am one) are descendants of the tribe of spiritual leaders who served in the Temple in Jerusalem and did not receive land. In the book of Esther, we are told that Mordecai was an *ish Yehudi*, a Jew or Judean, in his case specifically from the tribe not of Judah but of Benjamin. In Esther, the term is one of proud self-reference, having been maintained and embraced long after 586 BCE when Judea ceased to exist politically.

In speaking about this curious appellation, my grandfather, Rabbi Ahron Soloveichik, once suggested that if we are proudly named for the tribe of Judah (whether or not we descend from him personally), it is because of the original Judah's great moment of repentance.

Recall: Among Jacob's twelve sons, Judah was the one who infamously came up with the idea of selling Joseph, their father's favorite son, into slavery. Many years later, this great sinner, standing before the current vizier of Egypt – that is, his disguised brother Joseph – puts his own life on the line by personally guaranteeing the life of their brother Benjamin, whom the unrecognized vizier cruelly demanded be left behind and enslaved.

Faced with the possibility that, if he were to abandon his brother Benjamin, he would be effectively perpetrating again the same crime he committed in the long-ago past, Judah, sinner and now penitent, betrayer and now savior, coward and now hero, does not flinch in offering his own life for his brother's – as if to declare, "He is my brother; I am responsible for him; his life is in my hands; I am Judah who betrayed my brother, and I say this."

And that is a deeper reason why we are all *Yehudim*: The appellation proclaims the essence of Jewish identity. Every Jew – be he or she of the tribe of Benjamin, or Levi, or for that matter any of the ten tribes of Israel, is a *Yehudi* because she or he is bound in that intimate, familial relationship of responsibility with every other Jew.

The late sociologist Robert Bellah, a keen student of American religious life, coined the phrase "the imperial republic of self" to capture how so many of his countrymen had taken to living solely for their own individual wants, needs, and desires. He cites the case of a young woman named Sheila who described her faith as "Sheilaism": just her own voice, telling her how to live for herself.

> "It is not whether the Jews will survive but whether you, Esther, will survive as a Jew by living up to all that the term Yehudi implies and demands."

Judaism, we might say, is the complete opposite of Sheilaism; it is a familial faith in which we are intimately bound up with other Jews, and which by its very name implies responsibility for and solidarity with other members of our family and our people.

Which brings us back to Esther, the person and the book. As mentioned earlier, the story occurs after the destruction of the First Temple in 586 BCE and the mass exile of the Jews to Babylonia and beyond, there to form the first large Diaspora in Jewish history. In the Persia of this biblical book, the Jews have become culturally assimilated. They have taken on Persian dress, Persian mores, and most shockingly, Persian names – Mordecai and Esther are two examples. It was in part thanks to those names that they were able to blend into and become so seamlessly identified with Persian society and to play important roles in the royal court.

Nor were the names Mordecai and Esther ordinary. At the Pergamon Museum in Berlin, one of the most cherished exhibits is the reconstructed gate of King Nebuchadnezzar, the conqueror of Judah and despoiler of Jerusalem. The gate is named for the Babylonian goddess Ishtar and dedicated to the god Marduk. It is these foreign gods from whom Esther and Mordecai's names are respectively derived.

Today, of course, Mordecai and Esther have become Jewish names. But for the classical Jewish reader of the Megillah, a deep tension would be felt in the way one of the book's heroes is introduced: "There was a Jew in Shushan the capital [or 'palace'], and his name was Mordecai." A Jew with the name of a pagan divinity? What is his *true* identity? Will he live up to the demands of loyalty and solidarity that the term *Yehudi* implies? And what about the Jewish woman named Ishtar, a woman so culturally assimilated that no one at court has guessed her identity? What is *her* true identity?

Esther will face the need to answer that question when, as a Jew, she is brought face-to-face with a stark choice: to save herself, or to risk her life for her people. At first, she hesitates. It is Mordecai "the Judah-ite" who urges her to act heroically and come out, as it were, as her true self. Protesting, she points to the danger: she cannot approach the king without explicit permission or invitation, and she has not seen him for a month.

Then, in one of the most stirring verses in the Bible, Mordecai informs Esther of the eternity of the Jewish people and, simultaneously, of their assuredly common fate. The question, he says, is not whether the Jews will survive but whether you, Esther, will survive as a Jew by living up to all that the term *Yehudi* implies and demands:

> Think not that you will be protected in the king's house apart from all of the other Jews. If you are silent at this time, sustenance and salvation shall arise for the Jews from another place. But you and your father's house will be lost. (Est. 4:13–14)

Rabbi Aharon Lichtenstein captured the emotional force of Mordecai's rebuke:

> Mordecai does not attribute her response to weakness. He pushes his assault all the way, appealing to the deepest recesses of the Jewish soul. He accuses Esther of refusing to plead their cause before the king not because she lacks courage, not out of weakness,

> but rather as a calculated choice: "Let the entire Jewish nation be destroyed. Let them all perish – young and old, men and women. I will remain secure in the royal palace." This is how Mordecai interprets her response, and this is what he addresses: not weakness, not a lack of courage, but rather... *apathy*. If you really cared, if you considered your own soul to be at stake, would you be able to say "for a whole month I have not been called to the king"? Is this how someone talks when she believes that her nation is in danger?[5]

This is the book's turning point. Esther's choice lies between active selfless solidarity with her people and passive refuge in what Robert Bellah calls the "imperial republic of the self." She chooses to act – with, as we have noted, a plan to bring about Haman's downfall – and to do so by rallying the support of her fellow Jews. "Go and gather all the Jews in the capital," she says to Mordecai. "Let them fast for me before I go in to see the king." It is by means of her own heroic example that the disparate Jews will become united, first in fasting for Esther and ultimately in the battle against Haman's forces.

▲
Haman Begging the Mercy of Esther, Rembrandt van Rijn

Through Queen Esther, Jewish solidarity is restored. And that is why the book of Esther is seemingly devoid of manifestations of the Divine. Of course divine providence still exists and is at work in a seemingly godless world; this, for Judaism, is axiomatic. The real question posed by the book of

Esther is whether, in an era of exile and assimilation, the Jewish people still exist *as* a people. When they are dispersed across an empire, when their names are pagan names, when their cultural affiliations are no longer Israelite affiliations, do they still feel a solidarity with and a responsibility for each other?

In brief, the Megillah removes theology from the picture in order to make a theological point. When the Divine seems absent, when the incentives for Jewish loyalty are nowhere to be found, the mystical and metaphysical bond among Jews can nevertheless make itself manifest. That is why the key rituals of Purim center not on prayer to God but on obligations to our fellow Jews, encapsulated in the mutual sending of comestibles and the giving of gifts to the poor.

The purpose of commemorating and celebrating the story of Esther is thus not only to rediscover the providential divine Director of history but, especially, to reawaken within us a deeper understanding of our identity as Jews. Purim reminds us that if a man named Marduk can first and foremost be and act as a Jew, if a queen of Persia named Ishtar can first and foremost be and act as a Jew, then no matter the trappings we may have taken on, the same is true of all of us as well: *we* are Jews, and we are bound to each other.

That is also the true explanation for one of the most famous – and most misunderstood – traditions of Purim: a tradition, relatively recent in Jewish history, that evidently dates to the fourteenth or fifteenth century. Walk the streets of a Jewish neighborhood on Purim and you will find them crowded with children, and some adults, dressed in comic and at times outrageous attire as they bustle to bear gifts of food to their fellow Jews.

It is often conjectured that the practice of costumes on Purim is in remembrance of Esther's initial hiding of her own identity. The truth, however, is the exact opposite. We wear costumes not to disguise our inner selves but rather to show that no superficial sartorial choice can affect that rock-bottom identity, the central defining aspect of ourselves. No matter what may be "disguising" us, we still act as Jews. We still read the book of Esther in the synagogue, and we still bring gifts of food to our fellow Jews and alms to the poor. It is our past, our story, that defines us.

Purim Feast, Moritz Daniel Oppenheim

And that is also what Purim *asks* of us: who are we really? A holiday marked by levity issues from a deadly serious premise: not only that Hamans exist in every generation, but also that our Jewishness binds us to one another whether we like it or not. Purim, in other words, is the holiday of Jewish solidarity.

Hence the ever-present question: Is that solidarity really real? Is it really real for *us*?

So often throughout Jewish history, after all, solidarity has been hard to come by. In his memoir *White Nights: The Story of a Prisoner in Russia* (1957), Menachem Begin describes his imprisonment by the Soviets during World War II for crimes that he allegedly committed as a Zionist. There, in Vilna's Lukishki prison, he becomes friends with two non-Jewish and non-Russian cellmates who confess to him that their deepest desire is for Hitler's Germany to attack the Soviet Union; then they would be released to fight for Poland. "Whatever the future holds in store for us, there is no doubt that if war breaks out between Germany and Russia, we'll get out of this stinking cage."[6]

Begin also wanted to be released. But who knew what would result if (as ultimately did happen) Hitler were indeed to attack the

Soviet Union, thereby placing multitudes of Jews and Jewish communities at the mercy of the Nazi hordes? Writes Begin:

> My reply burst, as it were, from my very heart: "Gentlemen, I can't share your delight. I also think that a trial of strength between Russia and Germany is inevitable.... [But] I can't forget that in the event of a Russo-German war, more millions of Jews are likely to fall into the hands of Hitler. And what will become of them? You maintain that war between these two will give us prospects of getting out of Lukishki. Yes, I also want to get out, but when I think of them I tell myself that if I have to be released at such a price, I would rather remain in Lukishki.[7]

The reply of the prisoners was an explosion of wrath:

> "What you have just said," asserted one of them, "is most characteristic. With you people, everything is decided according to one criterion: what is good for Jews. Actually I was told long ago that there is solidarity

Lukishki prison cells, photograph by Olga Posaskova

> among all Jews, but you have given me confirmation that you people guard your solidarity under all circumstances, even in prison." The other prisoner was equally angry. "The Jews always stick together," he said, "don't try to deny it. Why, you yourself have just said that it is better that we should all rot in this stench, if only no harm will befall your people."[8]

Begin, in his memoir, reflects as follows:

> What was there for me to reply to their contentions? They both spoke of Jewish solidarity as if it were a crime, as if they were talking about a conspiracy, something evil. For heaven's sake! – I thought to myself – what have the Jews not done to prove that they do *not* stick together? In every European war, except this last, the Jews of one country fought against the Jews of another.... What blood offerings the Jews have given on this altar, the altar of proof that Jewish solidarity does not exist...!
>
> And all to no purpose. The fictitious Jewish solidarity exists and will always exist – in the minds of others. And if this is the case – I asked myself – has the time not come to strip it of the slur of a crime, the accusation of a conspiracy? Is our fate not unique? And is it not common to all of us Jews? Has not the time come to convert Jewish solidarity from a Gentile myth into a Jewish reality?[9]

How true are those words of Begin: if only solidarity *were* a Jewish reality. And yet, from time to time, that solidarity does make itself manifest, revealing the identities that beneath our assorted cultural veneers bind us to each other. Perhaps the most wondrous aspect of the coming into being of the State of Israel was its unquestioned, reflexive ingathering of Jews from all over the world and from vastly different societies and cultures, Jews who looked different and who spoke differently from their fellow Jews.

To the theologian Michael Wyschogrod, indeed, what allowed the State of Israel to come into being was precisely the Jewish familial ties that transcended culture and borders. In his words,

> Out of people of the most diverse cultural and national traditions, Israel created one people. To be more accurate, it did not create such a people but found one in existence. In the early stages of the Zionist movement, European Jews had little acquaintance with Sephardi Jews.... As the movement developed... it became clear that non-European Jewry would constitute a large segment of the state's population. Yet the viability of a state made up of such diverse elements was never brought into question. There was a bond among Jews that was deeper than all differences, differences that turned out to be far more superficial than would have been thought.[10]

"Perhaps the most wondrous aspect of the coming into being of the State of Israel was its unquestioned, reflexive ingathering of Jews from all over the world."

Four decades later, Natan Sharansky, the once five-year-old boy whom the events of Purim 1953 had saved from Stalin's clutches, would, like Menachem Begin, be placed in a Soviet prison for the "crime" of Zionism – an event that helped to spur a movement that united American Jews on one side of the world with their sorely beleaguered brethren on the other. Today, in an age marked regularly by Jewish fragmentation, it is easy to look back wistfully at those times, when Jewish unity was something that, at least at moments, could be truly felt.

Sharansky, who spent nine years in the Soviet Gulag before being freed in 1986, was once asked by a reporter to reflect on "how the Soviet Jewry movement was a catalyst for Jewish self-discovery not only inside the Soviet Union but perhaps for just as many people who were living comfortable lives in the West. There's nostalgia for this moment now."[11]

Sharansky, ever quick to respond with humor, picked up on the unconscious irony of the word "nostalgia" when applied to his nine-year ordeal:

> Well, of course it was a great time. And a few years after I was released, when I was playing with my daughters in my yard, our neighbor, who made *aliya* from America some years before, looked to me playing with my daughters and with a very nostalgic sigh she said, "Natan, it was such a great time when you were in prison. We all were going to demonstrations, we had our dates, we had our twinned bar mitzvahs [of American youngsters with their Soviet counterparts], we were all friends. Where did it all go?"
>
> I almost apologized to her for being out of prison. But I have no intention of going back. The Jewish people will have to find other reasons to love one another.[12]

The enemies of the Jews remain. Cultural assimilation flourishes. Internal fissures persist. And we do have to find reasons to love one another – something that will occur only if we come to appreciate the indelibility of Jewish identity. To that end, there is no better path than by relearning the story that connects us all. It is a story abundant with wondrous episodes. In discovering what those episodes are, and who we are, the book of Esther is a very good place to start.

Chapter Seven
Passover

The Ten Commandments, movie poster (1956)

In 1956, millions of Americans flooded into their local theaters to see the story told in the biblical book of Exodus brought to life in Cecil B. DeMille's *The Ten Commandments.* Among the moviegoers were American Jews who could not help feeling that the film spoke, personally and profoundly, to them. Some of these Jews – refugees and survivors who in the post-World War II years had only recently joined American society – were no less aware, however inchoately, of the deep connection between their own faith and the cultural ideals and self-conception of their new home.

Indeed, that connection was reinforced by the film's prologue, in which DeMille himself appeared on screen and addressed the audience directly. "Ladies and gentlemen," he began, "this may seem an unusual procedure, speaking to you before the picture begins." And then he defined the message, as he saw it, of the film about to be screened:

> The theme of this picture is whether men ought to be ruled by God's law or whether they are to be ruled by the whims of a dictator like [the Egyptian Pharaoh] Rameses. Are men the property of the state, or are they free souls under God? The same battle continues throughout the world today.

For most American moviegoers in the 1950s, and all the more so for recent Jewish immigrants who had survived the Nazi Holocaust or managed to escape Soviet-dominated Eastern Europe, it was hardly necessary for DeMille to spell out just whom he had in mind by invoking "a dictator like Rameses" or by referring to places where citizens were "the property of the state" versus places where they were "free souls under God." Nor was it any exaggeration for DeMille to suggest that the biblical story of the Exodus from Egypt lay at the heart of America's own idea of freedom.

Today, however, in our contemporary culture, the link between the biblical and the American conceptions of freedom has been severed. In 2014, almost six decades after the premiere of DeMille's film, a radically transfigured remake of the Exodus story was released. Produced and directed by Ridley Scott, *Exodus: Gods and Kings* gave us, in the biting summary of the critic John Podhoretz, "Moses as an insurgent lunatic terrorist with a bad conscience; the pharaoh who sought the murder of all first-born Hebrew slaves as a nice and reasonable fellow; and God as a foul-tempered eleven-year-old boy with an English accent."

It would be hard to imagine a more thorough travesty of the Exodus itself, not to mention the significant role played by the Passover story in American culture. And that is but one reason why both need to be recovered. For in truth, the Festival of Freedom has at least as much to teach us today as it did when *The Ten Commandments* was screened in 1956.

At that time, Americans were well aware of the phrase the "four freedoms," enunciated during World War II by Franklin D. Roosevelt as centerpieces of democracy that people "everywhere in the world" deserved to enjoy. The list – freedom of worship, freedom of speech, freedom from want, freedom from fear – was, and remains, praiseworthy. But there are other freedoms, first given to the world by Judaism, that are now more urgently relevant than ever.

The central ceremony through which Passover is celebrated is the Seder, a Hebrew word meaning "order" or "arrangement": a sequence of recitations and rituals spaced around the drinking of four cups of wine. These four cups, according to the Jerusalem Talmud, testify to the four different verbs used in the biblical book of Exodus in describing the Almighty's redemption of the Israelite slaves. Indeed, throughout the Haggadah – the text through which the successive stages of the Seder unfold – the number four can be found frequently, not only in the four cups and the four verbs but also in the four questions, the four sons, and still others. In what follows, I mean to propose that the festival of Passover also teaches us about another four *freedoms* – the significance of which, like the significance of the Exodus story itself, needs to be rediscovered.

The first of the four freedoms is freedom through children.

The Seder ritual itself, almost in its entirety, is focused on children, and many of its constituent parts originate in the deliberate intention to spark the curiosity of the young. Throughout the Seder, the story of the Exodus is told, retold, and reenacted in such a way as to speak not only to the child's intellect but also to his or her imagination. Although most Jewish festivals are similarly experienced at home and in the family setting, only Passover, the Festival of Freedom, *obliges* us to focus first and foremost on the pioneer generation.

But what, one might ask, do children have to do with freedom? In a personal sense, is it not true that the more children you have, the *less* free you become? An old joke describes a father with his little son at a supermarket. The child is having a meltdown, and the father responds in a soothing voice, "Okay, David. Stay calm, David. We'll be home with Mommy soon, David." A nearby woman shopper says to the father, "Sir, I just want to say how impressed I am by your patience with little David here." The father looks at her and replies, "Madam, *I'm* David."

Similarly, if you were planning to create a meal in the course of which you would discuss the most serious of subjects – what Passover is all about, the origins of the Jewish people, the nature of freedom, the purpose of the covenant – would your first thought be, "Let's do it with the kids"? The Seder has often been inaccurately compared to a Greek symposium: a gathering to discuss intellectual subjects over wine. As described most famously by Plato, these events featured scholars and statesmen, physicians and philosophers, and their students and disciples. Not one of them ever brought his children along.

The Seder, by contrast, is all about children. We begin with them posing seemingly simple questions to us, and we are obligated to answer without regard to the questioners' level of learning or maturity, be they wise or wicked, simple or too inexperienced even to ask. The very source of the obligation to tell and retell the Passover story year after year, to celebrate the Seder year after year – indeed, the very source of the Hebrew word *haggadah*, "the telling" – lies in Moses's instruction to Israel on the eve of the Exodus from Egypt: "And you shall *tell* your child on this day" (Ex. 13:8). For rabbinic Judaism, Moses has bound all subsequent generations to connect their progeny with the events that occurred to their ancestors.

> "If freedom were only for ourselves, in the here and now, then the Seder's celebrations and commemorations would have nothing to do with our posterity."

For that reason, according to Jewish law, should your grownup recitation and discussion at the table drag on, causing the children to fall asleep and thus miss most of the ritual, you will have failed in your obligation. To put it bluntly: the ritual is not about you; it is about them.

Why would the Seder be performed in this way? An answer can be found in a political distinction that we owe to the American founder Thomas Paine – namely, the distinction between society and state or government. In the opening to his famous 1776 pamphlet *Common Sense*, Paine put it this way:

> Some writers have so confounded society with government as to leave little or no distinction between them; whereas they are not only different but [also] have different origins. Society is produced by our wants, and government by our wickedness; the former promotes our happiness positively by uniting our affections, the latter negatively by restraining our vices.

The text of the Haggadah is focused on children because freedom obligates us to build up our society before focusing on our polity, and our society cannot be built if the next generation has no notion of our origins, our founding story, and the values we hold dear. In the words of Rabbi Jonathan Sacks:

> Reading the Bible, you would think that Moses, on the eve of the Exodus, would speak to the Israelites about politics, policy, nationalism. But he speaks instead about children: "On this day tell your son, I do this because of what the Lord did for me when I came out of Egypt." Moses fixed his vision not on the immediate but on the distant future, and not on adults but children. In so doing he was making a fundamental point. It may be hard to escape from tyranny, but it is harder still to build and sustain a free society.[1]

If freedom were only for ourselves, in the here and now, then the Seder's celebrations and commemorations would have nothing to do with our posterity. It is only through their *transmission* that our liberties can be kept alive. If what we are marking is first and foremost the freedom of a people, of its society, and of all it holds dear, then these can be preserved only if our future is bound to our past.

In his first public speech, known as the Lyceum Address (January 1838), Abraham Lincoln fretted that the tale of American independence, and the memory of the ideals of liberty in whose name it was secured, would be forgotten. That invaluable gift could be preserved, Lincoln went on to argue, only if the story of the liberation, and what it was for, was renewed in American society from generation to generation. Immediately after the 1776 revolution, he reminded his audience,

> a living history [of its ideals] was to be found in every family in the form of a husband, a father, a son or brother [who had fought for American independence] ... a history, too, that could be read and understood alike by all. But what an invading foeman could never do, the silent artillery of time has done. They are gone.... They were the pillars of the temple of liberty; and now that they have crumbled away, that temple must fall – *unless we, their descendants, supply their places with other pillars* [emphasis added].

Hence, on Passover, the focus on children, on the linking of freedom to children, and on transmitting to them our most sacred beliefs and traditions by recounting the story of the Exodus. Just as society (in Thomas Paine's formulation) precedes the state, so culture precedes politics. Ensuring the perpetuation of our values is what makes the perpetuation of political freedom valuable in its own right.

And that leads to the second Jewish notion of freedom: freedom not as an end in itself but as a means to an end.

For Judaism, redemption from physical shackles was only the beginning. And because in Judaism the theological is linked to what is arguably the most important factor in our everyday existence – namely, the food we eat – it is worth considering a Hebrew name given to Passover, the Festival of Freedom. It is *Ḥag HaMatzot,* the Festival of Matzah, the bread of freedom.

How odd. Which bread would seem worthier of being affiliated with the notion of freedom: plain unleavened matzah, or deliciously risen challah? We must delve further into the difference between the two to understand why matzah represents freedom.

Leavened bread is dough that has been allowed time to rise and thus to achieve its ultimate end; matzah, for its part, is bread in the first stage of its production, flour baked immediately after water has been added to it. Thus, Rabbi Yoel Bin-Nun suggests, matzah symbolizes the idea that the exodus from Egypt is only the beginning of the process of redemption, with a long hard road through the desert and thereafter through the millennia of our people's story, with the final chapter yet to come.[2]

> "Which bread would seem worthier of being affiliated with the notion of freedom: plain unleavened matzah, or deliciously risen challah?"

This same notion lies at the heart of remarks delivered in April 1944 by Lieutenant General Mark W. Clark, commander of the United States Fifth Army, as he addressed American Jewish soldiers attending a Seder in Naples, Italy. "Tonight," the general said,

> you are eating unleavened bread just as your forebears ate unleavened bread. Because the exodus came so quickly, the dough had no time to rise. There was [also] a time of unleavened bread in this [current] war... when it looked as though we might not have time to rise – time to raise an army and equip it, time to stop the onrush of a Germany that had already risen. But the bread has begun to rise... and the victory will be ours.[3]

This same unrisen bread of freedom figures centrally in a brilliant device to capture the attention of children. Many Sephardic Jews precede the reading of the Haggadah with a reenactment of the Exodus in which a seder celebrant, with no differentiation as to age, places a matzah on his or her back and is asked, Where are you from? "I am from Egypt," comes the reply. Another question is asked: Where are you going? And the answer: "I am journeying to Jerusalem." Then other Seder celebrants join the journey.

This homespun tradition beautifully embodies both of the first two freedoms: freedom through children – a first step toward the future – and freedom not as an end in itself but as a journey toward something in that future. The Jewish Festival of Freedom is about linking our ancestry to our posterity, our founding to our future.

And so to our third revolutionary conception of freedom: freedom in time.

In the 1993 movie *Groundhog Day*, Bill Murray plays a cynical and selfish weatherman by the name of Phil Connors. We come upon Phil as, on February 1, he arrives in the Pennsylvania town of Punxsutawney for the celebration of a famous groundhog (also nicknamed "Phil") who, every year on February 2, emerges from hibernation to "predict" either an early spring or six more weeks of winter. The next day, after covering the festivities, treating the locals rudely, and enduring a blizzard that makes travel out of town impossible, Connors falls asleep in his motel, only to awaken the next morning to discover that time has stopped. It is once again February 2, and the radio is blaring: "It's Groundhog Day."

And that is merely the beginning. Morning after morning, the time loop continues, driving Connors to distraction, violence, and attempted suicide – until, finally, having come to know in intricate detail everything that happens in Punxsutawney on February 2, he focuses on using every minute toward a moral purpose: fixing flat tires, restoring life to those who have narrowly escaped death, learning to love. Having at last lived a morally perfect day, he wakes up the next morning, and it is February 3.

This is an allegory for our age; it is also the story of the origins of our people, the tale of the Exodus. For the morally and spiritually enslaved, every day is the same. In utter contrast is the Festival of Freedom. Why does it imbue us with the need to ensure that our children relearn the tale of our liberty, and why does it emphasize that freedom is not an end but a beginning? Because, as Rabbi Soloveitchik argues,

> truly to live in time, to feel time's rhythm, is to feel the obligation to move from the memory of the past to the unreality of the future...from events that were and are no longer toward that which will be real someday – from reminiscing to anticipating. To live in time means to be committed to a great past and to an unborn future.... Man, according to Judaism, should try to mold and fashion the future. That is exactly why he has been created as a free agent.[4]

In this way, Rabbi Soloveitchik concludes, "Jews cherish the fleeting moment as if it represented eternity. Every year is valuable. Every second is precious."[5] Every moment can determine the course of our lives, and of the Jewish people.

We are now able to understand another curious aspect of the Festival of Matzah: namely, the removal from our homes of all traces of what the Torah calls *ḥametz*. The term refers not only to bread that has been allowed to rise but to all other forms of leaven as well. That is why preparing for Passover begins weeks earlier in the laborious process of cleaning house, removing leaven, and checking for still more leaven lest it be found after the holiday's onset. Many Jews even set aside a bit of *ḥametz* and burn it just before the holiday.

What does the obligation to rid ourselves of

"Dance of Marian," ▶ *Golden Haggadah*

leaven – even to incinerate it – symbolize? What does *it* have to do with freedom?

The answer, my grandfather suggested, lies in the Torah's insistence that as free men and women we are obligated to spend our time wisely. For how does *ḥametz* come about? By letting dough just sit there. It is a symbol, thus, of procrastination, of the idle passing of time, of putting off till tomorrow what we ought to have done today, of ignoring our ideals, of delaying our dreams, of letting precious time go to waste.

This can be seen most directly in the use of the verb form of *ḥametz* in one of the most famous talmudic phrases: *Mitzvah haba'ah leyadkha al taḥmitzenah,* "Whenever you have an opportunity to perform a mitzvah, a commandment, don't let it 'leaven.'" And that is why, once a year, we rid ourselves of *ḥametz*. We remove it from our homes because year after year we forget this lesson of liberty: freedom is inextricable from a proper approach to time.

Passover Seder, *Barcelona Haggadah*

"Many human beings," wrote Rabbi Joseph Soloveitchik, "float on the tide of time because there seems to be no alternative; time, for them, is an all-powerful, irresistible force." But true freedom is to be the master of our time. Matzah, bread baked quickly, not allowed to sit, not allowed to ferment and leaven, is for us akin to becoming masters of time: now we are getting a new start, inspired to live life with alacrity and to give every bit of time the attention it deserves, for it is all too apt to slip through our fingers. This freedom is what the medieval Christian theologian Thomas Aquinas and his later interpreters called "freedom for excellence": building on the past in becoming the people we are called to be.

And that brings us to the fourth and perhaps the most counterintuitive freedom of all: freedom through law.

"The paradoxical fact is that one consequence of our redemption from slavery has been… an enormous number of rules for our behavior."

As we've seen, the very word for the Passover celebration, *seder*, means order – and order is exactly what is needed for this most intricate of celebrations. Indeed, the laws of Passover occupy more pages in the corpus of Jewish legal codes than are devoted to any other holiday. The paradoxical fact is that one consequence of our redemption from slavery has been… an enormous number of rules for our behavior.

This was hardly lost on the authors of the Haggadah itself, who articulate it through the question posed by the wicked son. What, he asks, is this labor that you are undergoing? All of this preparation, this exertion, this obligation – *this* is freedom?

It is not a foolish question; it is an obvious one. Less obvious is the answer given to the wicked son by the Haggadah: "It was for the sake of *this* that God acted for me in taking me out of Egypt." In other words, the Haggadah flips the entire story of Passover on its head. It is not so much that we eat matzah in order to remind us of the Exodus. Rather, the Exodus occurred *so that* we could eat matzah. The purpose of freedom was the observing and fulfilling of the rituals of Judaism.

It is this concept – today so baffling at best, so alienating at worst – that we must comprehend. Interestingly enough, it often resonates most with thoughtful and sympathetic individuals on the outside of traditional Judaism looking in.

A number of years ago, I accompanied *The New York Times* columnist David Brooks on a tour of the Pomegranate supermarket in

Brooklyn, New York, a deluxe grocery emporium for Torah-observant Jews. Struck by the role played by law in ordinary, everyday Jewish life, he wrote the following in a column about his experience:

> [A] really impressive thing about the store is not found in one section but is pervasive throughout. That's the specialty products designed around this or that aspect of Jewish law. There are the dairy-free cheese puffs in case you want to have some cheese puffs with a meat dish, precut disposable tablecloths so you don't have to use scissors on the Sabbath.... Pomegranate looks like any island of upscale consumerism, but deep down it is based on a countercultural understanding of how life should work.
>
> Those of us in secular America live in a culture that takes the supremacy of individual autonomy as a given.... You choose your own path.... For the people who shop at Pomegranate, the collective covenant with God is the primary reality and obedience to the laws is the primary obligation.[6]

When Brooks asked me to explain the role of this "primary reality" in Jewish life, I referred him to a passage in which the Catholic writer George Weigel, quoting a modern scholar, distills in contemporary terms the thought of Thomas Aquinas:

> Freedom is the capacity to choose wisely and to act well as a matter of habit or as an outgrowth of virtue.... It's a bit like learning to play a musical instrument. Anyone can bang away on a piano; but that is to make noise, not music, and it's a barbaric, not humanistic, expression of freedom. At first, learning to play the piano is a matter of some drudgery.... But as our mastery grows, we discover a new, richer dimension of freedom: we can play the music we like, we can even create new music on our own. Freedom, in other words, is a matter of gradually acquiring the capacity to choose the good and to do what

> we choose with perfection. Law is thus intertwined with freedom. Law can educate us in freedom. [7]

That the rules imposed by religion can actually help make us more free, however countercultural this may seem today, is something America did once instinctively understand – and practice. The French diplomat and historian Alexis de Tocqueville, in his 1835 masterpiece *Democracy in America,* was powerfully impressed by exactly this aspect of American social and political reality, which was so alien to his native experience:

> In France I had almost always seen the spirit of religion and the spirit of freedom marching in opposite directions. But in America I found they were intimately united and that they reigned in common over the same country.[8]

This union of "the spirit of religion and the spirit of freedom," de Tocqueville explained, owed to the fact that although in America religion "takes no part in the government of society... it must nevertheless be regarded as the foremost of the political institutions of that country; for if it does not impart a taste for freedom, it facilitates the use of free institutions."[9]

Or, as the American political analyst Yuval Levin has formulated the same point, the American founders understood that

> religious institutions are not just counterbalances but foundations of the liberal order. They command us to a mixture of responsibility, sympathy, lawfulness, and righteousness that aligns our wants with our duties. They help form us to be free. They are foundational to liberalism not so much because they counteract its vices as because they prepare human beings to handle the burdens and responsibilities of being free.[10]

This, then, is the meaning of the Haggadah: for the sake of the law, God took us out of Egypt. The Exodus was for the law, for without the law we are not free. While practitioners of religious faiths built on laws are often derided as trapped and *un*free, it is they and they alone who have not been swept away by the tides of time. For those who have endured, freedom is understood not merely as the dissolving of fetters for individuals in the here and now but as the linking of parent and child, generation to generation, and as a journey toward excellence. For them, law is not the opposite of freedom; it is conducive to freedom. Correlatively, this is a freedom that, in controlling and sanctifying time, flourishes under law.

Freedom through children, freedom as a beginning and not an end, freedom in time, freedom through law: these are the four freedoms expressed in the Passover celebration, in the Seder that is built around four cups, in the Haggadah featuring four sons, in our answers to the four questions, and in the holiday celebrating the story that gave these four understandings to America's conception of itself.

Once, Jews seeking freedom brought that story with them to American shores. It is little known that Cecil B. DeMille's 1956 movie *The Ten Commandments* was a remake of a silent-film version that DeMille himself had produced in 1923. To serve as extras playing the Israelites in that earlier film, he hired several hundred Orthodox Jews who had freshly arrived from Eastern Europe. (Only a year later, America's doors would begin to close and severely limit further mass immigration.) For the filming of the Exodus scene, DeMille set up a gigantic replica of the gates of Egypt in the California desert, not far from the shores of the Pacific.

Although the immigrants were not trained actors, they did not need to act.

Many decades later, quoting liberally from contemporary sources, the journalist Marshall Weiss would recreate the scene. Citing the reporter Hallett Abend in *The Los Angeles Times,* Weiss writes:

> These Jews streamed out of the [set's] great gates with tears running down their cheeks, and then, without prompting or rehearsal, they began singing in Hebrew the old chants of their race, which have been sung in synagogues for thousands of years.

The Ten Commandments: TK (1923)

Weiss continues:

> According to syndicated Hollywood columnist Jack Jungmeyer [who was present at the filming], the Jews chanted "Father of Mercy" [*Av HaRaḥamim*] and "Hear O Israel" [*Shema Yisrael*]. He heard one of the older Jews say to a crew member, "We know this script – our fathers studied it long before there were movies. This is the tale of our beginnings. It is deep in our hearts."
>
> An elderly woman, overcome with emotion, fell to her knees and shook a fist at the gates of Pharaoh, weeping and casting sand on her head....
>
> For the scene depicting the parting of the sea, actor Theodore Roberts as Moses stood on a rock at the Pacific shoreline, surrounded by the children of Israel. As sunset approached, clouds blocked out the light, threatening to ruin the shot.
>
> "Just then the clouds cleared," Abend wrote. The nearly level rays of the sun made a halo around the figure of the prophet, giving a startling radiance to his face."

> "A gasp went through the crowd," [writer Rita] Kissin recalled. "The faces of men and women reflected this light. Tears trembled on wrinkled cheeks, sobs came from husky throats. For many, the world had moved back 3,000 years, and they stood once more on the shores of the Red Sea, viewing once more the good omen of deliverance."
>
> Most of the Jews, immigrants from Eastern Europe, didn't speak English. Yet, for them, the silent *Ten Commandments* was more than a movie. Playing the roles of their ancestors in the exodus was emotional for them and the others on the set; during those moments, *the American dream and their heritage converged* [emphasis added].[11]

Today, the Exodus conception of freedom no longer converges so smoothly with the values of American culture. In our prosperous republic, the four freedoms of FDR are still remembered, but the four freedoms of the Seder have largely been lost. If our free society is to flourish, they must be recalled. Passover, at the dawn of spring, urges and inspires us to learn them again.

CHAPTER EIGHT

Israel Independence Day and Jerusalem Day

The most recent additions to the annual cycle of religious celebrations are Yom HaAtzma'ut (Israel Independence Day) and Yom Yerushalayim (Jerusalem Day), the latter marking the moment when the Old City of Jerusalem was captured in the Six-Day War of June 1967. These are, in one sense, similar to the other holidays in the calendar, but in another sense they are profoundly different.

In order to understand why Jews celebrate these brightest moments in recent history, we begin with one of history's blackest.

April 1945 was the month in which the Holocaust came to a close. On April 11, a Wednesday, the concentration camp of Buchenwald was liberated by General George Patton's Third Army. As the Americans approached the camp, many inmates, inspired by the prospect of liberation, ran for the gates, triggering a hail of gunfire from the remaining Nazis in the guard tower. A young boy with the Yiddish nickname of Lulek was in the shooters' line of sight; suddenly, someone jumped on him and held him down until the firing ceased. As the Americans entered the camp, Lulek got up, ran away from his savior, and cowered behind a pile of corpses.

Accompanying Patton's soldiers was a chaplain named Rabbi Herschel Schacter. According to a retrospective article in *The New York Times*, published upon the rabbi's death in 2013, this was the scene that greeted him:

> There, in filthy barracks, men lay on raw wooden planks stacked from floor to ceiling. They stared down at the rabbi, in his unfamiliar military uniform, with unmistakable fright.
>
> "*Shalom Aleichem, Yidden,*" Rabbi Schacter cried in Yiddish, "*ihr zint frei!*" – "Peace be upon you, Jews, you are free!" He ran from barracks to barracks, repeating those words....
>
> As he passed a mound of corpses, Rabbi Schacter spied a flicker of movement. Drawing closer, he saw a

> small boy, Prisoner 17030, hiding in terror behind the mound.
>
> "I was afraid of him," the child would recall long afterward.... "I knew all the uniforms of SS and Gestapo and Wehrmacht, and all of a sudden, a new kind of uniform. I thought, 'A new kind of enemy.'"
>
> With tears streaming down his face, Rabbi Schacter picked the boy up. "What's your name, my child?" he asked in Yiddish.
>
> "Lulek," the child replied.
>
> "How old are you?" the rabbi asked.
>
> "What difference does it make?" Lulek, who was seven and the youngest survivor of Buchenwald, said. "I'm older than you, anyway."
>
> "Why do you think you're older?" Rabbi Schacter asked, smiling.
>
> "Because you cry and laugh like a child," Lulek replied. "I haven't laughed in a long time, and I don't even cry anymore. So which one of us is older?"
>
> Rabbi Schacter took the boy by his hand and made the rounds of the barracks, announcing the liberation: "*Sholem Aleichem, Yidden,* you are free!"[1]

Five decades later, this youngest survivor of Buchenwald, whose actual name was Israel Meir Lau, would become the chief rabbi of the State of Israel: one of many instances of how, out of the ashes of the European Holocaust, a people built a country that is a beacon of democracy and a wonder of our age.

In a vision described in the biblical book of Ezekiel millennia ago, the Hebrew prophet is shown a valley filled with parched skeletons that, suddenly, take on physical flesh and then the spirit of life. "These bones," Ezekiel is informed,

> are the whole house of Israel: behold, they say, "Our bones are dried, and our hope is lost: we are cut off altogether." Thus saith the Lord God, "Behold, O My

▲
Rabbi Israel Meir Lau visiting Auschwitz (2015, photo courtesy of Sam Churchill)

> people, I will open your graves, and cause you to come up out of your graves, and bring you into the land of Israel. And ye shall know that I am the Lord."

This same passage in the book of Ezekiel served as the source for *HaTikvah*, which would become Israel's national anthem. In response to the ancient Israelites' plaintive cry, *Avdah tikvateinu*, "Our hope is lost," Jews would instead sing, *Od lo avdah tikvateinu*, "Our hope has *not* yet been lost." And indeed it has not. Jews today are witness not merely to an extraordinary moment in history but to a fulfillment of biblical prophecy.

To commemorate the creation of Israel and the restoration of Jerusalem as holidays in the Jewish covenantal calendar is thus to declare that Jews will forever remember these events because through them, God's chosen people experienced His hand in history. Like Tu BiShvat, or Hanukkah – two holidays that evolved over time – I believe that the two modern days of Jewish celebration will evolve from their present childhood to more formalized forms within religious Zionist communities. They already share one liturgical practice in common: On these days, many Jews recite Hallel, the series of psalms offering gratitude to God for His miraculous salvation. Toward the end of these psalms comes the verse, "This is the Lord's doing; it is marvelous in our eyes" (Ps. 118:23) – declaring that we have been witness, with our own eyes, and in our own age, to divine intervention.

"Each Jew," wrote the late Milton Himmelfarb, "knows how thoroughly ordinary he is; yet taken together we seem caught up in things great and inexplicable. It is almost as if we were not acting but being acted through."[2] To celebrate the new Israel-oriented holidays is to see Israel's story as further proof that the Jewish people continue to be "acted through" in our own time.

How, then, is the story of modern Israel at once similar to but also different from the holidays we have previously discussed?

To remember the Exodus from Egypt, or the Israelites' journey through the desert, or the Hasmoneans' rededication of the Temple, or the defeat of Haman is to recall miraculous salvations for which we thank the God of Israel; in this, the new holidays are similar. They differ in one respect: The previous holidays invoke miracles achieved through the agency of biblical and post-biblical heroes, prophets, and priests who for the most part acted explicitly in the name of the God of Israel. By contrast, the two most recent ones invoke miracles achieved by Jews who did not necessarily act in God's name or may not even have believed in Him.

Consider the moments just before the birth of Israel itself. On May 14, 1948, David Ben-Gurion and his Zionist compatriots were poised to declare the first new Jewish commonwealth in almost two millennia. But they became bogged down in textual minutiae. Rabbi Fishman-Maimon, the representative of the religious Zionist movement, proclaimed himself unwilling to sign any Declaration of Independence that made no reference to the God of Israel. For his part,

Aharon Zisling, the secular head of the socialist party Mapam, asserted that he would not affirm the existence of a God in whom he did not believe. Imagine the strangeness of the moment: the British authorities were departing; Arab armies were mobilizing to attack; the fate of the entire Zionist project, the hopes and dreams of millions, hung in the balance; and the Jews were debating the existence of God.

It was Ben-Gurion himself who proposed a compromise: The Declaration would conclude by asserting the signers placed their trust in *Tzur Yisrael*, the "Rock of Israel." The phrase, which appears in the Jewish prayer book, was inspired by the biblical reference to God as *tzuri vegoali*, "my rock and my redeemer" (Ps. 19:15). In referring to the "Rock of Israel" while refraining from any explicit

Raising of the Ink Flag, photograph by Micha Perry (1949)

mention of divine redemption, the Declaration could be affirmed by devout Zionists who would take the phrase as alluding to the divine defender of the Jewish people and by atheistic Zionists who would take it as alluding to the flint-like resolution of the Israel Defense Force. The modern Jewish state was born by eliding the issue.

Of course, for those who today celebrate Israel Independence Day as a religious holiday, removing God from the Declaration by no means does away with God's role in the divinely directed drama that is Jewish history. Indeed, for people of faith, the events that preceded and followed Israel's declaration of statehood were in themselves so staggering as to be explicable only in terms of providence.

Item: Harry Truman, whom no one had ever expected to become president of the United States, overrode his hero, General George Marshall, in supporting and recognizing the birth of a Jewish state – and did so in part because of his relationship with a Jew named Eddie Jacobson with whom, decades earlier, he had run a haberdashery business.

Item: Joseph Stalin, whose anti-Semitism rivaled Hitler's for virulence, ordered the Soviet bloc at the United Nations to support the November 1947 plan for partitioning Palestine into two states, and then allowed the Soviet satellite Czechoslovakia to sell airplanes and arms to the nascent Jewish state.

Item: The Jews of the Yishuv (the Jewish community in pre-state Palestine), who were fighting against overwhelming odds, and who were confidently predicted by expert Western opinion to suffer not only defeat but possible annihilation at the hands of enemy Arabs, showed flint-like toughness in their heroic victory over the better-armed and numerically far superior Arab forces.

And so forth, and so on. "There has to be somebody bigger than you and me that put it all together," marveled the American astronaut Gene Cernan as he pondered from the surface of the moon the mystery of our universe's existence. Just so, sense can be made of this episode in the history of the Jews only if Someone Else was at work as well.

This proposition has been most eloquently expressed by two very different intellectuals of our time who separately made the same point. The first is Paul Johnson, the British Catholic historian whom we quoted earlier reflecting in 1998 that of the "over one hundred completely new independent states" that had come into existence since 1948, Israel was "the only one whose creation can fairly be called a miracle." In the same essay, Johnson recalled that, at the time, enlightened Western opinion was "virtually unanimous that the [infant] state would be crushed. That was assuredly the view of most governments and military staffs."[3] All in all, Johnson concluded, "Israel slipped into existence through a window that briefly opened, and just as suddenly closed. Once again, timing – or, if one likes, providence – was of the essence.[4]

"The second figure making the same point was Rabbi Joseph B. Soloveitchik, who for his part cited as evidence the tense drama leading up to that November 1947 vote in the United Nations to support two separate states in Palestine and the no-less-fraught drama in the following year to recognize the State of Israel. Writing in the 1960s, and confessing himself at a loss to name "any other concrete achievement of the United Nations," Rabbi Soloveitchik was "inclined to believe that the United Nations organization was created specifically for this [sole] purpose – in order to carry out the mission which divine providence had set for it."[5] Over the ensuing years, the international body's sordid conduct toward Israel would only reinforce the anomaly of its conduct in 1947–48.

▲ UN partition vote, November 1947

More positively, for Rabbi Soloveitchik, the miraculous nature of Israel's birth was reflected in the colors of the national flag. Its blue and white stripes were adapted from the tallit, the Jewish prayer shawl, whose fringes, according to the Torah, were intended to be composed of white threads with, at each corner, threads dyed sky-blue (azure). The white threads, Rabbi Soloveitchik explained, denote clarity, that which is self-evident. They bespeak the power of the human mind to perceive, to deduce, to investigate, and to innovate. But then there is *tekhelet,* blue, according to the Talmud the [color of the] furthest reaches of heaven itself, reminding us of aspects of existence that are barely grasped.

How appropriate, then, that these colors ultimately adorned the flag of the Jewish state. Zionism was predicated on the ability of the Jewish people to achieve even the impossible, and Israel is indeed an immense human achievement. At the same time, this flourishing modern democracy is also a sign of the presence of the Divine in our lives, and a reminder of the mystery of Jewish chosenness. That is why it is loved by many – and also why it is hated by many.

Indeed, to many Jews today, including even many Israelis, it is positively discomfiting to think that we are the vehicles of some larger plan – discomfiting even if, or perhaps especially if, we are to regard ourselves as the chosen instruments through which that larger providential plan has come into being. One is reminded in this connection of J.R.R. Tolkien's children's book *The Hobbit* (1937), in which the heroism of the central character, Bilbo Baggins, leads to the fulfillment of a legendary prophecy. With wonder, Bilbo exclaims: "Then the prophecies of the old songs have turned out to be true, after a fashion!" To this outburst, the wizard Gandalf replies:

> Of course! And why should not they prove true? … You don't really suppose, do you, that all your adventures and escapes were managed by mere luck, just for your sole benefit? You are a very fine person, Mr. Baggins, and I am very fond of you; but you are only quite a little fellow in a wide world after all![6]

The story of the Jews is about quite a little people who throughout time and still today have helped make the ancient prophecies "prove

▲
The flag of Israel

true." To mark Israel Independence Day as a holiday is thus to reflect not only on the miracle of Jewish endurance but also on God's mysterious connection to His chosen people: an idea so profound and all-embracing that quite often it has been disbelieving or discomfited Jews themselves who ultimately, in a flash of insight, have become its most ardent exponents.

And this brings us to the reason why, nineteen years after the establishment of the modern Jewish state, another tremendous event – the Jewish people's return to Jerusalem in the Six-Day War of June 1967 – became a holiday all its own, and why, among all the well-known photographs documenting the country's history, the most famous is an image not of military conquests, or of David Ben-Gurion declaring Israel's independence, or of Menachem Begin signing the 1978 Camp David accords with Egypt, or of any number of outstanding generals or artists or scholars. Instead, it is the image of three simple soldiers staring up from the Western Wall at the newly liberated Temple Mount in the conquered Old City of Jerusalem.

Decades later, the photographer, David Rubinger, was asked if he agreed that this was the best picture he himself had ever taken. He demurred. "A good photograph includes no unnecessary elements. But here there are all kinds of people in the background, half a head here, a quarter of a nose there.... It's an important photograph, but not a good one."[7] Fortunately, Rubinger allowed his personal judgment to be overruled.

The picture of the Israeli paratroopers at the Wall – so famous, so venerated, so universally beloved – has been frequently compared with Joe Rosenthal's equally stirring and venerated World War II shot of American marines hoisting the Stars and Stripes at Iwo Jima. But they are different. The inspiring power of the latter stems from the

Paratroopers at the Western Wall, photograph by David Rubinger (1967)

action that it illustrates: young men laboring together to pay tribute to all of the soldiers, sailors, and marines who risked and gave their lives to save civilization. In Rubinger's photo, by contrast, the emphasis is not on action but on its opposite, a sudden moment of complete inaction. Having achieved what would become the most famous Jewish military victory in two thousand years, the soldiers stand stock still before the Temple Mount, historic locus of Jewish national and religious aspiration. To cite again the felicitous phrase of Milton Himmelfarb, they seem to be not actors but wholly acted upon or through.

And that is precisely the image's magic. As Yossi Klein Halevi writes, Rubinger's photograph has appeal partially because of the humility it conveys:

> At their moment of triumph, the conquerors are themselves conquered.... Rubinger's photograph catches a precise historical moment: the return of the last two thousand years of Jewish history to the Zionist story. Many of the paratroopers identified themselves as Israelis first, Jews only a distant second; some weren't quite sure whether they identified as Jews at all. And yet it is at the Wall of all places, symbol of the quietism of exile, where secular Israelis became reconciled with their Jewishness. As one paratrooper put it, "At the Wall I discovered that I'm a Jew."[8]

Perhaps, Klein Halevi adds, the photograph's appeal lies in the way it captures the return not only of Jewish identity but also and more profoundly the Jewish God:

> Judaism posited a daring idea: that God's power and goodness would be revealed not only in the majesty of nature but in the messiness of history – and even more improbably, in Jewish history.... The reverence that many Jews felt toward the photograph of the paratroopers was the stunned realization...that skeptical secularism may not be an adequate way of

> understanding the Jewish story, that God may be real after all.[9]

And this may be another reason why many Jews mark as a separate holiday the day in 1967 when three Israeli soldiers stood in evident awe at the Western Wall. Jerusalem, as Norman Podhoretz once put it, reflects "the scandal of Jewish particularity"[10]; the uniqueness of one city in the history of the world testifies to the enduring nature of one people on this earth.

Thus does the Jewish link to Jerusalem go hand in hand with the mystery of Jewish eternity. Established as ancient Israel's capital when now-long-extinct empires bestrode the world, Jerusalem was the site toward which Jews everywhere faced in prayer through the ages, thereby binding themselves to each other as empire after empire sank into ruin. By continuing to lay claim to this bond, Jews reminded the world that, as the Zionist leader Chaim Weizmann said to Lord Balfour, prime minister of the United Kingdom, "We had Jerusalem when London was a marsh."[11] It was thus also because of the Jewish *return* to Jerusalem that what the city has represented was felt so profoundly by Jews all over the world. We celebrate the day not only because Jerusalem is central to our spiritual lives but also because it was at that moment, captured in David Rubinger's photo, that Jews in Israel and around the world felt at once the heroism of the Israeli infantry and the hand of God in our history.

To be sure, emotions have faded over the years, and in worrisome ways. In June 1967, Jews of all stripes flooded toward the Temple Mount. By 2017, the fiftieth Yom Yerushalayim featured a parade of religious Zionist youth but not even a single bareheaded male. The holiday is now for religious Jews, and even for them the clarity achieved on the original Jerusalem Day has faded. Klein Halevi again:

> Every day I drive to work from my home along the route where the paratroopers fought in June 1967.... Yet most mornings I am too preoccupied...to notice the view outside my window. [But then] I suddenly remember where I am...[and] ask myself what it is

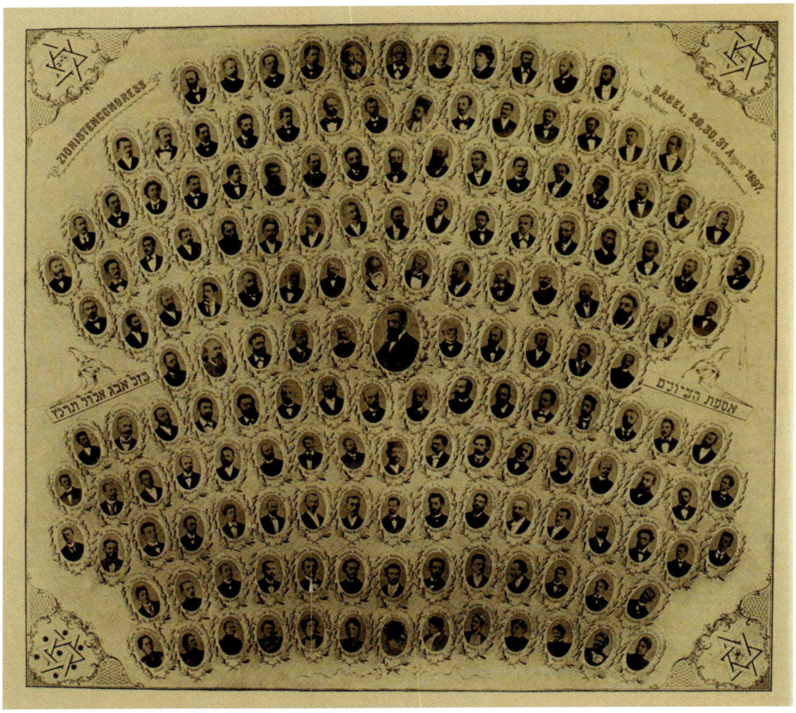

The First Zionist Congress, August 1897

> about this strange little people that continually finds itself at the center of international attention, repeatedly on the front lines against totalitarian forces of evil [that have] marked the Jews as their primary obstacle to achieving world domination. At those moments, I feel gratitude for having found my place in this story.[12]

The modern holidays of Israel's birth and the Jewish return to Jerusalem are a call to feel gratitude for finding our own place in this story, to recognize miracles in our time, and to ponder the meaning of these miracles for our faith and for the lives we live.

Along with the other surviving children of Buchenwald, Israel Meir Lau, the seven-year-old Lulek with whom we began this chapter, was placed by Rabbi Herschel Schacter on a transport to France. Reunited with his brother Naftali, he would make his way to Palestine, attend a yeshivah, and enter the rabbinate. Although he would always remember Rabbi Schacter, he had no idea who was the anonymous someone who protected him during the shooting and, by shielding this Jewish child, enabled him to encounter and be taken under the wing of the Yiddish-speaking chaplain.

As Rabbi Lau recounts in his memoir *Out of the Depths* (2011), the first major position for which he applied was as chief rabbi of the coastal city of Netanya. Interviewing for the job with city officials, the young rabbi encountered hours of questioning from Netanya's mayor and staff. Oddly, the deputy mayor, a man by the name of David Anilevich who should also have been deeply involved, sat on the side and said nothing.

As the interview came to a close, however, Anilevich stood up from his place and spoke:

> Friends, honored rabbi, before we disperse please allow me to say my piece. In a minute you will understand why I have been silent this whole time. I have been reliving April 11, 1945. I [had been] deported from my hometown to Buchenwald. On April 11, American airplanes circled in the skies above the camp. The prisoners, myself among them, were first out of the barracks. As we ran, a hail of bullets passed over us. Among those running toward the gate was a little boy.... I jumped on top of him, threw him to the ground, and lay over him to protect him from the bullets. And today I see him before me alive and well.[13]

Banging on the table so that all the glasses shook, Anilevich added:

> Now I declare this to all of you. I, David Anilevich, was saved from that horror, fought in the [elite Jewish force] Palmaḥ [in 1948], and today serve as deputy mayor of an Israeli city. If I have the merit of seeing this child, whom I protected with my body, become my spiritual leader, then I say to you that there is a God.[14]

The definition of a miracle is an event that should not naturally have occurred. In biblical history, the term tends to be applied to such events as the splitting of the Sea of Reeds, the stopping of the sun, the opening of the earth to swallow the rebel Korah and his band. By the same definition, as we have seen, it is a miracle that the State of Israel was born at all, and that it prevailed over its would-be destroyers. It is a miracle that, after a postwar generation in which many Jewish children grew up without parents, let alone grandparents, we have experienced the fulfillment of Zechariah's prophecy that grandparents would one day see their grandchildren at play in the streets of Jerusalem (8:4). It is a miracle that after so many civilizations have disappeared from the earth, Jewish children continue to be born. It is a miracle that as anti-Semitism today continues to haunt the nations of Europe, and has spread alarmingly into key American institutions, religious Judaism flourishes in the State of Israel. More than any other event in the last hundred years, that state – born, to repeat, in conscious avoidance of any explicit affirmation of Israel's God – stands as the greatest argument for His existence.

> "It is a miracle that the State of Israel was born at all, and that it prevailed over its would-be destroyers."

The rituals and ceremonies of the holidays marking the seminal moments in Israel's history will undoubtedly evolve. But those who observe these days *as* holidays have joined the miracle that is Israel to all the other miracles that have punctuated and that will, we pray, continue to punctuate the story of the chosen people.

Chapter Nine
Shavuot

Rejoicing of the Law, Solomon Alexander Hart

One evening in 1663, the London socialite Samuel Pepys decided to check out the city's latest attraction: Jews who had just been allowed back into England for the first time since their expulsion in 1290, almost four centuries earlier. To get a sense of this foreign community, Pepys sought to find a typical synagogue service. Unfortunately, the evening he innocently selected for his visit happened to coincide with Simḥat Torah, the fall festival when Jews rejoice – with raucous dancing – at the completion of the annual reading of the Torah, the Five Books of Moses.

"But, Lord!" the shaken and disgusted Pepys would afterward write in his diary,

> to see the disorder, laughing, sporting, and no attention, but confusion in all their service, more like brutes than people knowing the true God, would make a man forswear ever seeing them more and indeed I never did see so much, or could have imagined there had been any religion in the whole world so absurdly performed as this.[1]

Pepys's visit may have been ill-timed, but he did witness the soul of Judaism alive and (so to speak) kicking. For Jews, the Torah, the Law, with all of its commandments, is the source of the most profound joy. But while Simḥat Torah is indeed a venerable tradition, the true celebration of the Torah takes place not in the fall but in the late-spring festival of Shavuot, which is the subject of this chapter.

In Judaism, the holidays known as the *shalosh regalim* – the three pilgrimage festivals of Passover, Shavuot, and Sukkot – are linked both to the agricultural cycle of the Holy Land and to covenantal moments in Jewish history. Thus, in the Bible, Shavuot, which means "Weeks," is so named in part because seven weeks are counted from Passover at the beginning of the spring to the moment when the fruits of the land are ripening. Therefore, another biblically based name for Shavuot is *Ḥag HaBikkurim,* the Festival of First Fruits, a holiday that is bookended in

Samuel Pepys

the fall by Sukkot, which (as we have seen in chapter 3) is also known as *Ḥag HaAsif*, the Harvest Festival.

But the agricultural theme is only one aspect of the holiday. Counting forward seven weeks from Passover on the fifteenth of Nisan brings us to Shavuot on the sixth of Sivan, thereby linking the former, the great Festival of Freedom, to a covenantal moment of shattering significance: the date on which the redeemed Israelites stood at Sinai, when the Almighty declared the Decalogue – the Ten Commandments – following which Moses ascended the mountain to receive from heaven the rest of the Torah's commandments.

This, for rabbinic tradition, is perhaps the central reason why we count the seven weeks between Passover and Shavuot: in deliberately connecting the two, we assert that the chief *purpose* of the Exodus from Egypt was to receive the law. Hence Shavuot in the liturgy is defined as *zeman matan torateinu,* the "time of the giving of our Torah." What is emphasized is not only the existence of the Torah but also the fact that it (like, one might say, the harvest) is a gift, a *matanah*. The Torah – that rigorous and complex legal system containing 613 commandments, to which the rabbis would later add a myriad of further applications and expansions – is for Jews

The Summer (Ruth and Boaz), Nicolas Poussin, 1660–1664

an exquisite source of happiness: the ultimate embodiment of the Almighty's love for His chosen people.

Speaking for all Jews, the psalmist describes the study of God's commandments as both intellectually invigorating and spiritually exhilarating:

> The Torah of the Lord is perfect, restoring the soul; the testimony of the Lord is sure, making wise the simple; the statutes of the Lord are right, rejoicing the heart; the commandment of the Lord is pure, enlightening the eyes. More to be desired are these than gold, even much fine gold; sweeter also than honey and the honeycomb. (Ps. 19:8–11)

Thus declares David in the book of Psalms. Indeed, one explanation for the widespread practice of eating dairy meals on Shavuot derives from another culinary allusion, this one in the biblical Song of Songs: "Sweetness drops from your lips, O bride; honey and milk are under your tongue" (4:11). The talmudic rabbis applied this phrase metaphorically. The Torah, they averred, is milk and honey under our tongue. As Rabbi Aharon Lichtenstein once noted, milk is basic to a child's growth and necessary to its health while honey, something sweet, is a luxury. To speak of the Torah as both milk and honey is to say that it is simultaneously a crucial prerequisite to our existence and the greatest imaginable luxury. Nothing is more necessary; nothing is more delightful.

To an outsider, it may seem counterintuitive, if not outlandish, that something as complex and didactic and overtly burdensome as Jewish law could actually be a source not only of gratitude but of joy, not only of obligation but of exhilaration. Indeed, Christian thinkers far more thoughtful than Samuel Pepys have been taken aback by this aspect of Judaism, startled by the idea that law – in all its multifarious details – can be a source of delight.

Thus, in his 1958 *Reflections on the Psalms,* C.S. Lewis admitted to being confounded by the verses describing the Torah as sweeter than honey:

▲ C.S. Lewis, *Reflections on the Psalms* (1958)

> This was to me at first very mysterious. I can understand that a man can, and must, respect these statutes, and try to obey them, and assent to them. But it is very hard to find how they could be, so to speak, delicious, how they exhilarate.[2]

Indeed, Lewis wrote sharply, for a person striving to overcome his own desires in obedience to God's commands, the law "could be more aptly compared to the dentist's forceps, or the front line, than to anything enjoyable or sweet."[3]

In the past two decades, however, a number of sensitive Christian writers have expressed a new appreciation of this same Jewish love of the law. In what follows, therefore, our survey of the traditions and liturgies of Shavuot will benefit from the thoughts not only of rabbis, Jewish philosophers, and medieval and modern masters of Jewish literature but also of Christian theologians, a Supreme Court justice, and even an archbishop. Thanks to all of them, we will emerge with a truer grasp of what is meant by Shavuot as the time of the giving of our Torah.

We begin with a short story by the great Yiddish writer Yitzhak Leibush Peretz (1852–1915). In it, a hasidic leader or rebbe fails to show up for prayers during the penitential season preceding Yom Kippur. The reason, his followers speculate, must be that he has ascended to heaven to plead for mercy on behalf of his flock. In town, a Jew of Lithuanian origin (a "Litvak"), known to be of a decidedly less mystical bent than his hasidic brethren and instead devoted first and foremost to the minutiae of Jewish law, scoffs at this suggestion. According to the Talmud, he reminds them, even Moses himself, when he ascended Mount Sinai to receive the Torah on Shavuot, was barred from actually entering heaven.

Setting out to stalk the rebbe, the Litvak follows him to the outskirts of town. There, in a shack, lives a poor woman, elderly, blind, and feeble, whom the rebbe has been feeding and caring for. From that point on, writes Peretz, the once-cynical Litvak becomes a follower of the rebbe. Whenever anyone in the hasidic community asserts that he can be found in heaven, the Litvak responds: "If not higher."

Note well Peretz's literary maneuvers. He does not make the Litvak into a Hasid – i.e., one who thinks that a truly righteous man escapes our earthbound existence and enters into saintly transcendence. Instead, for the Litvak, a hovel can be holy. No act exists in a vacuum; rather, humans have the power to sanctify – to endow earthly existence with the glory of God through the performance of His will. If Judaism contains divinely dictated laws that relate to every aspect of human existence – not only how we treat the elderly but also what foods we eat, how and whom we marry, how we conduct business, how we farm, how we build a home, how we put phylacteries on our arms and fringes on our clothes, how we live every aspect of our lives – it is because we thereby elevate and sanctify every aspect of the world below.

This, incidentally, is the true meaning of the words *tikkun olam*, a phrase mistranslated as "repair of the world" and all too often mistaken as synonymous with American progressive politics. The actual words, which come from the *Aleinu* prayer, denote the Jewish aspiration to "adjust the world" through recognition of God's kingship, an aspiration achieved first and foremost through the applications of the *mitzvot* to every part of existence.

Jews do believe in heaven, and heaven is inherently holy. But it is what we do here below that turns this world into something "higher" than heaven itself. If heaven is a realm of celestial beings, we of flesh and blood can do something of which the angels are incapable: we can bring the sanctity of heaven to previously profane parts of our earthly lives. Just as, in Judaism, every realm of human life has its laws, so every aspect of physical reality is to be neither avoided nor transcended, but rather sanctified.

This point is captured in a talmudic tale (Shabbat 88b) about what occurred on the first Shavuot:

> As Moses ascended Sinai, the ministering angels spoke before the Holy One, blessed be He: "Sovereign of the Universe! What business has a human being among us?" He answered them: "he [Moses] has come to receive the Torah." They replied: "That secret treasure – You desire to give it to flesh and blood?!"
>
> "Give them a reply," said the Holy One to Moses.... Moses then spoke before Him: "Sovereign of the Universe! The Torah which You give me, what is written in it? 'I am the Lord your God, Who brought you out of the land of Egypt'" (Ex. 20:2).
>
> [God] said to the angels, "Did *you* go down to Egypt; were you enslaved to Pharaoh? Why, then, should the Torah be yours? Again, what is written in it? 'You shall have no other gods' (Ex. 20:3). Do you dwell among peoples who engage in idol worship? Again, what is written in it? 'Remember the Sabbath day, to keep it holy' (Ex. 20:8). Do you perform work, that you need to rest?... Again, what is written in it? 'You shall not murder. You shall not commit adultery. You shall not steal' (Ex. 20:13–15). Is there any jealousy among you; is the evil Tempter among you?"
>
> Straightaway the angels conceded to the Holy One, blessed be He. For it is said, "O Lord our Lord, how excellent is Thy name in all the earth" [Ps. 8:1] and not "[How excellent is Thy name] upon the heavens."

The Talmud here (as Rabbi Soloveitchik comments in his masterwork *Halakhic Man*) is saying that the Lord's name is made great when His will is actualized on earth; Jews seek not to escape the world but to elevate and ennoble it. The ideal of Jewish law (in Hebrew, halakhah) "is the redemption of the world not via a higher world but via the world itself.... [A] lowly world is elevated through halakhah to the level of a divine world."[4] If we in the modern age tend to think that Judaism consists of the synagogue and the prayers offered in it, the truth for Rabbi Soloveitchik is almost the opposite:

> The Judaism that is faithful to itself,...which brings the divine presence into the midst of empirical reality, does not center about the synagogue. These are minor sanctuaries. The true sanctuary is the sphere of our daily mundane activities, for it is there that the realization of Jewish law takes place.[5]

From this perspective, every obligation, every law, every single "Thou shalt" uttered by the Almighty is not daunting but delightful, another affirmation that every sphere of life can be made holy. Indeed, for Sephardi Jews, a longstanding centerpiece of the celebration of Shavuot has been the reciting of masterpieces of Hebrew literature known as *azharot*, "exhortations": a poetic medium in which giants of medieval Hebrew verse like Shlomo ibn Gabirol encapsulated, in rhymed stanzas, all 613 commandments of the Torah. Sung in the synagogue, the *azharot* celebrate each of the 613 as a precious gift bestowed on Shavuot.

The fact that 613 seemingly didactic commandments have been rendered into poetry – the fact that legal minutiae are not simply recited but *sung* – makes manifest what C.S. Lewis could not grasp. If the book of Psalms describes the law as a delight, it is in part because the law brings God Himself into every aspect of our lives.

In contrast to Lewis's bafflement, the contemporary Christian thinker Russell Reno praises Rabbi Soloveitchik for helping him understand why Jews see the Torah "as a gift and not a burden":

Shavuot, Moritz Daniel Oppenheim

> The all-encompassing array of divine imperatives – *mitzvot* – are as countless arrows of love shot downward and into human life. The more expansive and detailed the law, the more deeply and completely halakhic man's life is penetrated by the divine.[6]

Reno's description of the *mitzvot* as "countless arrows of love shot downward from heaven" captures the spirit behind the rabbinic formula recited at the end of a communal session of Torah study:

> Rabbi Hanania son of Akashia said: The Almighty wished to make Israel worthy; He therefore gave them an abundance of Torah and *mitzvot*. For it is written: "The Lord wished to ensure His people's righteousness; He increased their Torah that He may be glorified."

Through law, our lives are sanctified, and the world in which we live is rendered higher than heaven.

This is why not only the Ten Commandments but all 613 are such a source of celebration on Shavuot, including through the custom of staying up late, and in some cases until dawn, studying. Today no communal observance of Shavuot is complete without such a study session proceeding at least until late evening. It has become, essentially, one of the central rituals, if not the central ritual, by which the holiday is marked, either on one's own or by attendance at lectures.

In common parlance, this activity is called "learning Torah." But is that not an odd way of putting it? Imagine a Supreme Court justice of the United States taking down from the shelf one of his old law school textbooks and reading it. Can one say the justice is *learning* law, as if for the first time? Surely not. Yet were a rabbi to take in hand a talmudic tractate – one he has studied tens of times – and delve into it again, *learning* is the only way he would refer to the exercise. On Shavuot, we all do it.

"Through law, our lives are sanctified, and the world in which we live is rendered higher than heaven."

A blessing said daily by traditional Jews thanks the King of the Universe who "has sanctified us and commanded us to engage with words of Torah" and who "teaches Torah to His people Israel." In keeping with this invocation, anyone who studies the Torah seeks not merely to review what has already been learned but rather to glean something new, and to be taught something new.

The "learning" passion thus applies to the expert as much as to the novice. The Talmud itself is so vast precisely because rabbis over the centuries have examined and debated every word, every letter, every law, deducing new ideas, insights, and legal applications. This activity was founded on and justified by the conviction that the Torah, the gift of God Himself, is a window into His infinite mind.

"Turn it over and over," as one rabbi puts it in the Mishnah – that is, examine it thoroughly – "for all is in it" (Avot 5:22).

At it happens, this same mishnaic statement has the distinction of being the only one ever named in a decision by the U.S. Supreme Court – cited not by a Jewish justice but by the late Antonin Scalia, a Catholic admirer of the Jewish penchant for learning. Dissenting from the tendency of other justices to invent constitutional "maxims," he wrote:

> A talmudic maxim instructs with respect to Scripture: "Turn it over, and turn it over, for all is therein." Divinely inspired text may contain the answers to all earthly questions, but the due-process clause [in the fifth and fourteenth amendments to the Constitution] most assuredly does not.

Scalia's point was both witty and profound. The American Constitution is a human document, democratically adopted; we have no authority to discover new ideas within it. But if learning Torah is an engagement with the infinite mind of God, then even as the law is eternal, new insights can always be discovered, and by means of these insights we engage, as it were, with God Himself.

This experience, too, is a source of the delight described by David in the book of Psalms, the delight that C.S. Lewis did not understand but that has been recognized and appreciated by other outsiders to Judaism. Thus, a number of years ago, a group of cardinals and archbishops visited the study hall at Yeshiva University, where hundreds of students sit and "learn" Talmud together in pairs. One of the visitors, Archbishop Charles Chaput of Philadelphia, was so impressed by the scene that he delivered a homily about it in his own cathedral:

> What struck me first was the passion the students had for the Torah. They didn't merely study it; they consumed it. Or maybe it would be better to say that God's Word consumed them. When a man and woman fall in love, a kind of electricity runs not just between

> them, but also in the air around them. The story of every true encounter with God is the same…. I saw this in the students at Yeshiva.[7]

This electric spark is indeed part of why the Torah is greater than gold and sweeter than honey. And Archbishop Chaput also noticed something else fundamental to Judaism – namely, the way that engagement with Torah connects Jews not only to God but also to themselves and to each other. "God's Word," he said in his homily,

> is a living dialogue between God and humanity, and that divine dialogue mirrored itself in the learning dialogue among the students. The students began as strangers, but their work in reflecting on Scripture and in sharing what they discovered with each other created something more than themselves: a friendship between themselves and, beyond themselves, with God.[8]

To this I would add that the friendship is not only among those in the immediate vicinity, in the here and now. At the first Shavuot, those assembled around the mountain included not only the Israelites of the Exodus but the souls of all the Jewish generations. As the Torah has been learned in every generation, and transmitted to every generation, we unite with those generations when we learn what has been learned before us and passed on to us.

And not only that. Late in life, Rabbi Soloveitchik attended a celebration of the birth of a baby boy whose father and grandfather had been his students. Reflecting on what it means to have taught several generations, he described how he himself, in delivering a lecture to young students, felt as if all the sages of yesteryear had entered the classroom as well:

> I enter the class in a very pessimistic mood, and I ask myself, can there be a dialogue between an old teacher and young students?… [But] whenever I start the lecture, the door opens, and another old man walks in and sits down. He is older than I am. All the students

> call me the Rav, but he is older than the Rav. He is the great-grandfather of the Rav; his name is Reb Chaim of Brisk.... Then the door opens quietly again and another old man comes in; he is older than Reb Chaim, he lived in the seventeenth century.... And then more visitors show up. Some lived in the eleventh century, some in the twelfth century, some in the thirteenth century, some lived in antiquity. [Maimonides] says something, then another medieval sage, [Abraham ibn Daud], disagrees.... A boy [in the class] jumps up to defend [Maimonides], and the boy is fresh so he uses improper language. So, I correct him.... Another boy intervenes, and suddenly a symposium of generations comes into existence.
>
> We all speak one language, this march of centuries, this dialogue between antiquity and present.... We belong to the same community of transmission, where generations meet, where hands, no matter how wrinkled and parchment-dry one hand is and how soft and warm the other hand is, shake, unite, in a community where the great dialogue continues.[9]

Suggested by all of these thoughts is that the Torah ultimately connects us not only with ancient Israel and Moses who stood at Sinai, but also with the future, with babies newly born and as yet unborn. For if the Torah contains limitless insights waiting to be found, God will provide Jews to discover them. The Torah's infinity guarantees Jewish eternity.

This is what Jews celebrate on Shavuot, what someone as wise as C.S. Lewis could not take in, what other thinkers outside of Judaism are beginning to appreciate – and what some lost Jews have also discovered.

One representative of this last category was the writer Stephen Dubner, a son of Jewish parents who converted to Catholicism and raised their children in their newfound faith. Returning to Judaism as an adult, Dubner published a memoir of his journey entitled *Turbulent Souls: A Catholic Son's Return to His Jewish Family.* In it he describes how, early on, having reluctantly agreed to attend a synagogue, he instantly regretted his decision upon arriving. The synagogue was small and dimly lit, and no one prayed in unison; each congregant chanted to himself in incomprehensible Hebrew.

"What was I doing here?" Dubner wondered. "I felt at least like an intruder, perhaps an imposter, and I was utterly forlorn." But then the Torah was brought out.

> Suddenly all the jabbering was reduced to an appreciative murmur. The air itself seemed to grow lighter, easier to breathe. The bulky Torah scroll, swaddled in its glittering cover like a child of royalty, was liberated from the ark and escorted down the aisle by an old man struggling happily beneath its weight, and as the men and boys up front hurried to greet it, pressing the fringes of their prayer shawls to its cover and then kissing the fringes, I tumbled into a deep understanding. I, too, threw myself at the Torah, awkwardly scraping it with my fingers, lifting my fingers to my lips. A resonance – a gratefulness, a relief – blistered its way inside me.[10]

"Hope," Dubner concludes, "came to rest inside me. The way a Jew greeted the Torah – as though it contained everything he would ever need, everything that had ever been known or could ever be known."[11]

Turn it over, turn it over, for all is in it. That is why we celebrate Shavuot, and what it means to speak of the Torah as such a gift. It is on Shavuot that we celebrate the treasure more glorious than gold and sweeter than honey, cherishing it, studying it, learning it, and calling to our fellow Jews to join us and partake of the symposium of the generations: the one that began at Sinai and continues onward into eternity.

CHAPTER TEN

Tishah BeAv

In late July 1977, Menachem Begin, then newly elected as the prime minister of Israel, arrived in the United States to meet with President Jimmy Carter and the leadership of American Jewry.

Having previously lost more elections than any opposition leader in any democracy ever, Begin had recently succeeded in undoing the decades-long hold on government exercised by Israel's socialist establishment. Hence, for him, this visit marked a moment of long-awaited political triumph. And yet, peculiarly, one of the high points of his American stay was an event permeated with the spirit not of celebration and victory but of profound sadness and national defeat.

The reason: Begin's trip coincided with the ninth day of the Jewish month of Av, a day known by its Hebrew name as Tishah BeAv.

An evening-to-evening day of fasting and mourning, Tishah BeAv commemorates the destruction of the ancient Temple in Jerusalem, first by Nebuchadnezzar of Babylonia in 586 BCE and then, centuries later, by Vespasian and Titus of Rome in 70 CE. A prevalent custom at worship services on the evening and morning of the day is to spend the first part sitting close to the floor, exactly as Jews traditionally do during the *shiva* week following the death of a close relative. And so, as he joined the other congregants at an evening service on July 23, the new prime minister lowered himself to the synagogue floor and followed along with the chanting of *Eikha*, the biblical Book of Lamentations, ascribed to the prophet Jeremiah. In anguished and wrenching detail, the book recounts the devastation of the Temple and of the holy city of Jerusalem.

This was surely something that no previous or more secular prime minister of Israel had done or would have been likely to do. To the many reporters covering Begin's visit, moreover, the sight could only have appeared utterly incongruous: here was the leader of a *restored* Jewish commonwealth – and since 1967, a reunited Jerusalem – sitting *shiva*, as it were, for a city and a civilization that had been destroyed almost two millennia earlier.

"On July 23, the new prime minister lowered himself to the synagogue floor and followed along with the chanting of *Eikha*."

For anyone who knew Menachem Begin, however, his presence that evening was entirely apt. Tishah BeAv is first and foremost a day of mourning for the Temple itself, whose loss ruptured the intimate relationship of the Jewish people with the God whose presence dwelled in Jerusalem. Only with a longed-for rebuilding of the Temple could that special relationship be restored. But in Jewish history, much more than the Temple came to be mourned on that date, which over the centuries became accepted as a national "Memorial Day" marking successive occurrences of anti-Jewish violence and persecution.

Among these episodes were: in 135 CE, the crushing of Beitar, the final redoubt against the Romans that was held by the forces of the rebel leader Shimon bar Kokhba; in the Middle Ages, the active sanctioning of the Crusades by successive popes, with the aim of liberating Jerusalem from the hands of its Islamic overlords – a cause that provided legions of European Crusaders with a pretext for wreaking havoc, destruction, and mass murder in Jewish communities along the way; the 1492 expulsion of the Jews from Spain; and other catastrophic events, some of them specific to local Jewish communities, leading up in modern times to the genocidal onslaught on the entire Jewish people in the Nazi Holocaust.

If any prominent Jewish figure in modernity could be said to have fully internalized this history of Jewish persecution, that figure was Menachem Begin. And that is how the diplomat Stuart Eizenstat, who served as a policy adviser in the Jimmy Carter White House, described him, in the process succinctly articulating how many other American Jews must also have regarded the new Israeli prime minister:

> Begin had the familiar look of the Eastern European Jews of my grandparents' generation. He was almost completely bald, wore thick glasses, and had a protruding jaw and a face with a sad look that to my eyes made it appear he was carrying the traumas of the Jewish people in Europe through the ages.[1]

Menachem Begin, you might say, was the complete "Tishah BeAv Jew" – a burden, and for him a privilege, inscribed in his persona, in his bearing, and in his very language. Indeed, in his own recounting of the destruction by the Nazis of the Jewish community of Brisk, the Lithuanian city in which he had been born and raised, Begin reached back across a millennium of persecution to echo the resonant, despairing cry of another Menachem – the liturgist Menachem bar Machir – whose requiem for the German Jews massacred by Crusaders is still recited today among the many other *kinot*, poetic elegies, that make up the annual service on Tishah BeAv.

Each verse of Menachem bar Machir's poem ends in an alternating expression of profound personal grief: *Al'lai li,* "Alas for me!" or *Oya li,* "Woe is me!" That same haunting refrain also ends a deceptively plainspoken dirge by his twentieth-century namesake:

> Five-hundred Jews were led one day to the banks of the Bug River near Brisk, a mother-city of the Jewish

> people. Among them was my father. On the way, he started to sing the "song of faith": "I believe with unbroken faith in the coming of the messiah." He also called on the others to sing the Zionist anthem *Hatikva*, "The Hope." Everybody sang. The Germans pushed them into the river and opened fire on them. The Bug reddened from the blood of Jews. My father and teacher, my elderly father, was with them. *Oyah li!!*[2]

Linking one Menachem to another, the sanctified, centuries-old expression of woe becomes at one with the legacy of grief preserved and repeated by Jews year to year, era to era, as if to say that such mourning is a ceaseless exercise: a memorializing trust bequeathed from generation to generation that must never be permitted to lapse.

Of such stuff was this Tishah BeAv Jew made.

And yet: To see mourning as the essence of Begin's life, let alone the essence of Jewish life, would be radically incomplete. He received his own name, *menaḥem* ("consoler," also an epithet for the hoped-for Messiah), because he was born right after the ninth of Av before the "Sabbath of Consolation." And in fact, his lifelong refusal to forget the tragedies of the Jewish past went hand in hand with his fierce belief in Jewish endurance and his embodiment of an unswerving Jewish resolve.

That combination was on display when Begin appeared as a guest on the television show *Meet the Press* on the morning after his attendance at the Tishah BeAv service. (In contrast to the ritual laws governing observance of the Sabbath and other sacred days, one is permitted to work on Tishah BeAv.) Asked to say something about his recent meeting with President Carter, he disclosed that there was something more pressing that he wanted to address first:

Menachem Begin on *Meet the Press*, July 1977

> With your permission, before I answer this very important question, I would like to say a few words about the day we now meet on because of

> its universal importance. Today, in accordance with our calendar, it is the ninth of the month of Av. It is the day when 1,907 years ago the Roman Legions, the Fifth and the Twelfth, launched their ultimate onslaught on the Temple Mount, set the Temple ablaze, and destroyed Jerusalem, subjugated our people, and conquered our land. Historically, this is the beginning of all of the suffering of our people, dispersed, humiliated, and ultimately now a generation physically destroyed [by the Nazis]. We remember that day and now have the responsibility to make sure that never again will our independence be destroyed and never again will the Jew become homeless or defenseless.

For Begin, mourning was not only about the obligation to remember and never to forget the past but also about the ongoing duty to forge out of memory and mourning a positive guide to future action – a guide to how he himself must lead and a guide to how Jews themselves must live.

Here again one cannot imagine such a statement being uttered on American television by any previous Israeli prime minister. But in its light, we can also see one of the important differences between the ninth of Av and more familiar dates on the Jewish calendar like Passover and Yom Kippur. Uniquely, Tishah BeAv informs Jews how we are to exercise our collective memory not just on that day but continuously and throughout our lives. As such, and more than any other day on the Jewish calendar, Tishah BeAv encapsulates the essence of the Jewish approach to time, the meaning of Jewish memory, and the secret to Jewish eternity.

Let's explore this point.

In a scholarly essay published two decades ago, Jay F. Shachter provocatively suggested that certain rituals practiced by traditional Jews could easily strike outsiders as thoroughly weird, if not positively deranged. The essay was entitled "Case Study: Diagnosis and Treatment of a Psychotic Depressive."[3] To illustrate his contention, Shachter offered the example of *tikkun ḥatzot*, or "midnight mourning": a grieving ritual, performed by generations of mystically minded Jews not only on Tishah BeAv but throughout the year, which involves rising in the middle of the night to bewail the destruction of the Temple in Jerusalem.

Delving into a thought experiment – the "case study" promised in his title – Shachter imagines that an elderly observant Jew has been discovered by his assimilated American grandchildren as he engages in this act of mourning. Has their grandfather, they wonder, gone crazy? At their request, a modern secular psychiatrist who is the fictional author of Shachter's "case study" proceeds to examine this mourner of Jerusalem and to diagnose him as an individual suffering from severe mental problems. Here is the psychiatrist's summary of the case:

> The patients' grandchildren presented the author with a description of a unique and bizarre pattern of insomnia. According to the grandchildren's report, the patient would arise most nights at approximately midnight. The patient would then go to his fireplace, pick up some ashes, and put them on his forehead. Then he would sprawl underneath an open doorway with his face on the floor, muttering unintelligibly. The grandchildren reported that they had confronted the patient about this behavior, and that they had received the explanation that their grandfather was mourning for the Temple. It was at this point that the author received the initial contact….
>
> The patient obsessed over the loss of his "Temple," and he constantly hoped to get it back. In fact, it would not be an exaggeration to say that, for the patient, hoping to get back his "Temple" was a major reason for living. This "Temple" had been briefly lost once before, restored, and then lost again.
>
> On several occasions the patient's grandchildren told the patient in no uncertain terms that it was time for him to accept the loss of his Temple and move on.

> It was, after all, over one-thousand-nine-hundred years ago and the Temple was never going to be restored.... The patient, on the contrary, seemed to accept all his compulsions as completely natural, denied any distress over the control which they had assumed over his life, and was sincerely amazed that anyone would think one-thousand-nine-hundred years too long a time to wait for the restoration of the Temple.

Many and perhaps most traditional Jews do not observe a daily "midnight mourning." Yet all engage in similar activities on the ninth of Av. And, to the uninitiated, even the ritual on that day might well appear insane. Why actively and publicly mourn an edifice that was destroyed two thousand years ago? And as for the martyrs who throughout the generations died for their faith, why mourn them as if they died yesterday?

The question, and the answer, go to the heart of what Rabbi Soloveitchik dubbed Judaism's "very peculiar philosophy of memory." Mourning on Tishah BeAv and throughout the year is an outward sign of the Jewish ability, through ritual and study, to bridge those generations, to take a Jew back in time, to re-experience the trials and travails of one's ancestors, to refuse to allow them to die unforgotten. As Rabbi Soloveitchik puts it, memory in Judaism

"Why actively and publicly mourn an edifice that was destroyed two thousand years ago?"

> is not just the capacity of man to know events which lie in the past. Memory is experiential in nature; one does not simply recollect the past or just remember bygones but re-experiences that which has been, and quickens events that are seemingly dead.[4]

In this "unitive time consciousness," as Rabbi Soloveitchik calls it, "events in our history do not fade into antiquity but remain real, and ever-present." And that is what Tishah BeAv is all about. Jews do not randomly sit *shiva* for people who passed away centuries ago from natural causes. If they do "sit *shiva*" for the Temple, it is because for them, through memory, the Temple has just been destroyed. In the liturgy, as Rabbi Soloveitchik notes,

> we say, in the *kinot* [elegies]: "on this night, *beleil zeh*, my Temple was destroyed." *Beleil zeh* means now, tonight. Apparently, 1,900 years ago is neither remote nor distant from us; it is living… it is living.[5]

Two true anecdotes, and one undoubtedly apocryphal one, help bring the point home. The first is about Michal Avera Samuel, born in Ethiopia, who in 1984, as an eight-year-old, set out with her family and other Ethiopian Jews on a perilous trek through the desert to Sudan, from there to be transferred by airlift to Israel in the daring campaign known as Operation Moses. Today, Michal Samuel is a leading figure in the community of Ethiopian Israelis and works tirelessly for the betterment of Israeli society at large.

In a 2018 piece in the *Times of Israel*, Michal Samuel related an amazing fact: At the time of her childhood, many if not most of the Jews in Ethiopia had no idea that the second Temple had been destroyed. It was only after arriving in Israel, and experiencing Tishah BeAv for the first time, that they, and she, finally learned the news of Titus's conquest of the city two thousand years earlier. Their reaction? Rather than rejoicing in

Operation Moses: Ethiopian Jews arrive in Israel

the miracle of Jewish restoration, they wept for the Jerusalem that, to them, had just been lost. She writes:

> I grew up hearing about the *Kohanim* – the holy priests – and how they worked in the Temple. I fell asleep listening to stories about the halo hovering over Jerusalem.... My family and I, along with our neighbors from the Beta Israel community [in Ethiopia], hoped to merit to return to Jerusalem one day. We prayed, and performed customs that expressed our yearning for Zion.... The ideal of Jerusalem was the force that provided us with the stamina to persevere during the arduous trek through the desert [enroute to meet their Israeli rescuers].... We struggled to keep going despite the terrible conditions and the hunger, only because of our goal to reach Jerusalem of Gold and, after so many generations, stand at the gates of the Holy Temple. Then we arrived and discovered that the Temple had been destroyed.... Learning about the destruction of the Temple only as I reached the gates of the Old City was an earth-shattering disappointment, and it left a great void in me that I have been unable to fill.[6]

To arrive in the modern State of Israel and learn all of a sudden that the Temple is gone – it is hard to fathom the effect of such a blow. And yet, elsewhere in the same piece, the Michal Samuel of today tempers her picture of a "great void" with a more nuanced understanding of what the very "ideal of Jerusalem," as she herself calls it, gave her:

> Only upon maturing, and having overcome the struggles of integration into Israeli society, did I begin to understand how fortunate I was to have grown up believing that the Temple existed. I succeeded at forging my personality with the goal of being worthy of visiting the Temple!... I was fortunate to have had

> time stand still and experience this deep connection to a Temple that in our minds and hearts still existed, resonating within me for many years.[7]

Just so: for what is the observance of Tishah BeAv, rightly understood, meant to do, if not to turn all of us into Michal and her family – to mourn for Jerusalem as if it were just now lost to us, to be inspired by its ideals, to yearn for, and work toward, its restoration?

Which brings us to the second true story, this one told by a nineteenth-century non-Jewish eyewitness to the Jews' public mourning for Jerusalem.

William Seward, secretary of state in the presidency of Abraham Lincoln, visited the Holy Land upon his retirement from public service. Arriving in Jerusalem on a Friday, he was struck by the crowds of Jews streaming to the "Wailing Wall," as the Western Wall was then widely known, to recite the book of Lamentations before the onset of the Sabbath. In a memoir of the trip edited by his son, Seward describes the scene:

> For centuries (we do not know how many) the Turkish rulers have allowed the oppressed and exiled Jews the privilege of gathering at the foot of this wall one day in every week, and pouring out their lamentations over the fall of their beloved city, and praying for its restoration to the Lord....

The Wailing Wall, Gustav Bauernfeind (1887)

> The small rectangular oblong area, without roof or canopy, serves for the gathering of the whole remnant of the Jewish nation in Jerusalem. Here, whether it rains or shines, they come together at an early hour, old and young, men, women, and little children – the poor and the rich, in their best costumes, discordant as the diverse nations from which they come. They are attended by their rabbis, each bringing the carefully-preserved and elaborately-bound text of the book of the Lamentations of Jeremiah.... For many hours they pour forth their complaints, reading and reciting the poetic language of the prophet, beating their hands against the wall, and bathing the stones with their kisses and tears.... During the several hours while we were spectators of it, there was not one act of irreverence or indifference.[8]

Seward, deeply moved by the experience, heads this chapter of his memoirs with a biblical quotation: "Walk about Zion, and go round about her: tell the towers thereof. Mark ye well her bulwarks, consider her palaces; that ye may tell it to the generation following" (Ps. 48:13–14). In so doing, he offers a striking confirmation of Michal Samuel's insights a century later. For in quoting verses that are not about Zion in its destruction but about Zion in all its glory, Seward signifies his own deep understanding that, through the very process of mourning, Jerusalem comes to life once again.

Which brings us in turn to the almost certainly apocryphal tale that describes Emperor Napoleon passing by a synagogue on the ninth of Av. Hearing the cries and moans from within, he inquires what terrible tragedy has just occurred, only to be informed that the Jews are crying over the conquest of Jerusalem by the Romans 1,800 years earlier. His purported response: "A people that will never forget their city and Temple can never be destroyed."

Apocryphal or not, the lesson is true: the Jewish act of mourning – in actuality, an act of reliving – turns past into present. In so doing, it creates reality, and keeps Jewish identity itself alive. As Rabbi Soloveitchik once commented, if the destruction of the Temple did not destroy the Jewish people as well, the reason was that the Temple they built and preserved in their hearts, their spiritual Temple, was impregnable; against it, all the armies of Babylon and Rome proved utterly impotent. Similarly, if Jews dispersed throughout the world remained existentially linked to the land of Israel and to Jerusalem, the reason was that, in mourning its destruction and yearning for its restoration, they were still *there*.

Begin himself would express this same truth with pithy eloquence: although his childhood home was located geographically in Eastern Europe, spiritually he and other Jews all over the world had been, he said, "born in Jerusalem."

The way we respond to tragedy is the key to our triumph.

And yet, for many modern Israelis as for many leading Zionists prior to Begin, reality demanded a very different approach. To them, the birth of Israel meant forgetting the sadness and impotence of exile, deleting the memory of what occurred in the long centuries of exile and dispersion. Still today, around the time of Tishah BeAv each year, articles inevitably appear in the Israeli press arguing that, with the restoration of the Jewish state, Tishah BeAv serves no purpose. Besides, why should we be mourning when we have so much to celebrate?

To ask this question is to lose sight of what Tishah BeAv is. For Begin, as we noted early on, the insistence on commemorating the inflictions of the past and the refusal to forget were personal guides to how he would lead Israel and the Jewish people. If a prime minister of Israel still observed the day, it was because he understood that mourning the past does not in the least depreciate the miracles of our time. Quite the contrary, it makes them all the more vividly present. Moreover, by refusing to forget what occurred in our past, we arm ourselves against those who would harm us now.

Hatred of the Jewish people still haunts the world. On the Temple Mount, the holiest Jewish site on earth, haters of Jews deny the very existence of the Temples that once stood there and work to destroy any evidence of that existence. In Europe, the virulent species of anti-Semitism that was thought to have been eradicated for all time by the defeat of Nazi Germany has raised its head once again, not infrequently with homicidal results. Even in today's United States, hatred of Jews, sometimes thinly cloaked as hatred of Israel,

At the Entrance to the Temple Mount, Gustav Bauernfeind (1886)

has infected some of the highest places of civilized discourse in the land, prominently including American universities.

Jewish tradition tells us that one day, with the world redeemed, Tishah BeAv will cease to be a sad time for us. Until that day, even as we celebrate the miracles with which our own generation has been blessed – the miracles of the Jewish return to the Holy Land and to a reunited Jerusalem, the miracles celebrated in the holidays of Yom HaAtzma'ut and Yom Yerushalayim – we mourn because we owe it to the past to remember all that has been lost, to keep alive within us those who have come before – and to continue to dream, in the midst of mourning, of what might yet come to be.

That is also why, incongruous though it may appear after our chapter-by-chapter rehearsing of such thoroughly certified wonders as the triumphant Exodus from Egypt, the giving of the Torah at Sinai, the miraculous journey of Israel in the wilderness, and the later redemptions of Purim and Hanukkah, it is fitting to conclude this book with Tishah BeAv. For unless and until Tishah BeAv is grouped in tandem with the holidays of celebration, we will not have fully grasped what I have insisted is the greatest wonder of all: the wonder of Jewish endurance.

> "We mourn because we owe it to the past to remember all that has been lost, to keep alive within us those who have come before."

Our mourning kept Jerusalem and the Jewish generations alive within us, and our celebratory observance of previous salvations provided us with the certainty that we could experience miracles once again. Jay Shachter, in his "case study" of a seemingly insane elderly Jew who mourns a temple from 1,900 years ago, has his hypothetical psychiatrist reflect as follows:

> In all human beings there is a tendency toward health.... [P]eople experience loss, grieve, and eventually – though it may take a long time – recover. But there was an unusual factor in this patient's history.... He lost his Temple *twice*. In retrospect, this seems to be an event of crucial importance.
>
> However attached the patient had been to his Temple, had he lost it only once, it seems likely...that after one-thousand-nine-hundred years he would have done exactly what his family urged him to do: accept that it

> would never be restored, and move on. But there had been an earlier loss prior to the current one, following which the Temple had been restored. Because of this earlier loss, however brief it may have been, the patient acquired the *disabling delusion* that the current loss would be temporary as well.[9]

This perception is not without a kernel of truth. But was the aged patient, not to mention the ageless Jewish people, under the influence of a "disabling delusion"? Hardly. Because the Jews had witnessed miracles of redemption and salvation in the past, they believed ardently – and, as history records, accurately – that such miracles could recur. Just so, we who have experienced miracles in our own time can believe in similar miracles recurring in the future. In this sense, to mourn is to hope; to mark Tishah BeAv in sadness is never to give up on the happiness in the waiting.

There was once a prominent tradition among Jews to preface the weekday Grace After Meals with Psalm 137, "By the rivers of Babylon," in which the captive exiles from the destruction of the First Temple proclaim, "If I forget thee O Jerusalem, let my right hand forget its cunning." On Shabbat, however, the day understood to offer a foretaste of the redemption, that psalm was replaced with another: Psalm 126, the great hymn of thanksgiving sung by the Jews *released* from Babylonian captivity and returning to build the Second Temple. It begins: *Shir hama'alot beshuv Hashem et shivat Tziyon hayinu keḥolmim,* "A song of ascents: when the Lord returned us to Zion, we were as dreamers." The sequence from one psalm to the other links the mourning and memorialization of Jerusalem with the certain vision of Zion restored.

This, too, Menachem Begin understood. The man who in 1977 arrived in America to observe Tishah BeAv and meet with the nation's president would return to the White House two years later to sign the history-making peace accords between Israel and Egypt. For his remarks at that dramatic event, Begin as usual composed a draft and then turned to his speechwriter, Yehuda Avner, to "Shakespearize" it. But then, having seen Avner's polished draft, he abruptly decided to revert to his original handwritten version. In his book *The Prime Ministers,* Avner recounts their exchange:

> "You weren't happy with my changes?"
>
> "Oh, no, they're fine," [Begin] assured me. "It's just that as I was going over the typed text I suddenly had the feeling that today of all days I want to read my own speech exactly as I wrote it in my own hand."
>
> And to make the implicit explicit, he added, "I wrote it from the heart and I want to read it from the heart."[10]

It was indeed a speech – an extraordinary speech – from the heart. It began with soaring words about the occasion, and about the joys and beauties of peace; moved on to lofty praise of the "civil courage" displayed by Anwar Sadat, the Egyptian president, in embarking on his peace initiative with Israel and seeing the process through to a signed treaty; and concluded, electrifyingly, in these words, delivered (Avner writes) in a voice "husky with emotion":

> This is the proper place, and the appropriate time, to bring back to memory the song and the prayer of thanksgiving I learned as a child in the home of my father and mother, which doesn't exist anymore because they were among the six-million people – men, women, and children – who sanctified the Lord's name with their sacred blood that reddened the rivers of Europe from the Rhine to the Danube, from the Bug to the Volga, because – only because – they were born Jews; and because they didn't have a country of their own, or a valiant Jewish army to defend them; and because nobody – nobody – came to their rescue, although they cried out "Save us! Save us!" *de profundis,* from the depths of the pit and agony. That [song of thanksgiving] was the Song of Ascents, written two millennia and five-hundred years ago when our forefathers returned from their first exile to Jerusalem and Zion.[11]

At that point in his speech, Begin took out of his pocket a *kippah* and placed it on his head, intoned the opening verses of the great biblical psalm of thanksgiving – *Shir hama'alot beshuv Hashem et shivat Tziyon hayinu keḥolmim* – and continued to read onward in the Hebrew. "I will not translate it," he concluded his remarks. "Every person, whether Jew, Christian, or Muslim, can read it in his or her own language in the Book of Books. It is simply Psalm 126." For Jews in the audience and around the world, it was a moment never to be forgotten.

As we've seen, Menachem Begin was named Menachem because he was born before *Shabbat Naḥamu,* the Sabbath of Consolation that follows Tishah BeAv. The name could not have been more appropriate, for his legacy prominently includes the active and vital linking of the destruction that was with the miracle that is, and with the redemption that is yet to occur. Standing before the world at the White House in Washington, at the summit of his career, invoking the image of his parents in Brisk singing the hymn of thanksgiving and teaching it to their young child, he made it known that it was because of *their* loyalty to Jerusalem, at one with the loyalty of all

Menachem Begin and Anwar Sedat, March 1979

of the murdered martyrs of Jewish history, that the miracle of the return to Zion could actually occur in our time.

More than any other day in the Jewish calendar, it is Tishah BeAv that reflects how Jews will never forget, and therefore why – as Napoleon may or may not have said; as William Seward attested; and as Michal Samuel and countless generations of Jews have sensed from earliest childhood – the Jews as a people will never die.

Notes

Introduction

1 Rabbi Joseph B. Soloveitchik, *The Lord is Righteous in All His Ways: Reflections on the Tish'ah Be-Av Kinot* (Ktav, 2006), 201.

2 Rabbi Joseph B. Soloveitchik, *Out of the Whirlwind: Essays on Mourning, Suffering and the Human Condition* (Ktav, 2003), 17.

3 Rabbi Samson Raphael Hirsch, *Collected Writings*, vol. viii, part 4, (Feldheim Publishers,1995) 240.

4 Jacques Laskar, "Large Scale Chaos and Marginal Stability in the Solar System," *Celestial Mechanics and Dynamical Astronomy* 64 (1996): 146.

5 Fred Heeren, "Home Alone in the Universe?," *First Things: A Monthly Journal of Religion and Public Life* (2002): 38–47.

6 *From a letter to F. A. Van der Kemp [Feb. 16, 1809]* Founders Online, National Archives, htttps://founders.archives.gov/documents/Adams/99-02-02-5302.

7 Rabbi Samson Raphael Hirsch, *Collected Writings*, vol. viii, part 4, (Feldheim Publishers,1995) 240.

Rosh HaShanah

1 Rabbi Joseph B. Soloveitchik, *Family Redeemed: Essays on Family Relationships* (Ktav, 2000), 39.

2 Rabbi Joseph B. Soloveitchik and N. Helfgot, *Community, Covenant, and Commitment: Selected letters and Communications of Rabbi Joseph B. Soloveitchik* (Ktav, 2005), 296–302.
3 Leon R. Kass, "Educating Father Abraham: The Meaning of Fatherhood," *First Things* 48 (December 1994): 32–43.

Yom Kippur

1 Natan Sharansky, *Fear No Evil* (PublicAffairs, 1998), 363.
2 Ibid.
3 Stephen M. Barr, "Retelling the Story of Science," *First Things* (March 2003): 16–25.
4 *Mishneh Torah*, Repentance, ch. 5, halakhah 1.
5 https://www.sj-r.com/story/opinion/columns/2009/01/11/george-will-weep-for-death/43071513007.
6 C. S. Lewis, *Mere Christianity* (Zondervan, 2001), 56–57.
7 Ibid., 56.
8 Bernhard H. Rosenberg and Fred S. Heuman, eds., *Theological and Halakhic Reflections on the Holocaust* (Ktav, 1992), 54.

Sukkot

1 https://www.tabletmag.com/sections/food/articles/saved-by-cholent.
2 Ibid., 78.
3 C. S. Lewis, *Reflections on the Psalms* (Houghton Mifflin Harcourt, 1958), 79.
4 Rabbi Jonathan Sacks, "Judaism's Greatest Challenge," available at: https://www.rabbisacks.org/covenant-conversation/ki-tavo/judaism-greatest-challenge/.
5 Ibid.
6 https://www.theatlantic.com/magazine/archive/1961/11/the-secret-in-the-cliffs-the-discovery-of-the-bar-kochba-letters/657736.
7 Paul Johnson, *History of the Jews* (Harper & Row, 1987), 586.
8 Gil Marks, *Encyclopedia of Jewish Food* (Houghton Mifflin Harcourt, 2010).
9 Ibid.
10 Leon R. Kass, *Life, Liberty and the Defense of Dignity: The Challenge for Bioethics* (Encounter Books, 2002).
11 *Mishpacha*, September 11, 2013.

12 Jordie Gerson, *Forward,* October 12, 2016, https://forward.com/opinion/351835/this-sukkot-ditch-your-etrog-and-lulav-in-favor-of-apples-and-maple-leaves.
13 Matthew Kalman, "Seed of Extinct Date Palm Sprouts after 2,000 Years," June 12, 2005, https://www.sfgate.com/news/article/Seed-of-extinct-date-palm-sprouts-after-2-000-2628668.php.
14 *Commentary,* May 1998, https://www.commentary.org/articles/paul-johnson-3/the-miracle.

Hanukkah

1 *Slate,* December 3, 2007, https://slate.com/news-and-politics/2007/12/hanukkah-celebrates-the-triumph-of-tribal-jewish-backwardness.html.
2 *Mordecai M. Noah, Travels in England, France, Spain and the Barbary States in the Years 1813–14 and 15* (New York and London, 1819), appendix, pp. xxv–xxvi.
3 https://slate.com/news-and-politics/2007/12/hanukkah-celebrates-the-triumph-of-tribal-jewish-backwardness.html.
4 *The Ghetto and the Jews of Rome,* vol. 137 (Schocken Books, 1966), 20.
5 https://www.jewishvirtuallibrary.org/mark-twain-quotations-on-judaism-and-israel.

Tu BiShvat

1 Gil Marks, *Encyclopedia of Jewish Food* (Houghton Mifflin Harcourt, 2010).
2 Rabbi Berel Wein, https://www.yeshiva.co/midrash/15374.
3 Troy, Tevi. "I Think That I Shall Never See a Jew as Lovely as a Tree: How a Minor Day Became a 'Green' Blockbuster," *Commentary* 139, no. 2 (Feb. 2015): 25–29.
4 Ibid.
5 Ibid.
6 Ibid.
7 Mark Twain, *The Innocents Abroad* (American Publishing Company, 1869), 606.
8 Ibid.

Purim

1 https://etzion.org.il/en/holidays/purim/upside-down-world-megillat-esther.

2 Rabbi Jonathan Sacks, *A Letter in the Scroll: Understanding Our Jewish Identity and Exploring the Legacy of the World's Oldest Religion* (Simon and Schuster, 2004), 42.
3 Ibid.
4 Ibid.
5 *By His Light: Character and Values in the Service of God,* edited by Reuven Ziegler (Maggid Books, 2016), 152.
6 Menachem Begin, *White Nights: The Story of a Prisoner in Russia* (1957; English edition by Harper& Row, 1979), 46.
7 Ibid.
8 Ibid.
9 Ibid.
10 Michael Wyschogrod, *The Body of Faith: God and the People of Israel* (Jason Aronson, 1996), 240.
11 David Samuels, "A Fourth of July Story," *Tablet Magazine,* June 30, 2016, https://www.tabletmag.com/sections/news/articles/a-fourth-of-july-story.
12 Ibid.

Passover

1 Rabbi Jonathan Sacks, "Passover Tells Us: Teach Your Children Well," *Huffington Post,* https://www.rabbisacks.org/archive/passover-tells-us-teach-your-children-well.
2 Rav Yoel Bin-Nun, "On Chametz and Matzah," https://etzion.org.il/en/tanakh/torah/sefer-vayikra/parashat-tzav/tzav-chametz-and-matzah.
3 Bernard Postal, "A World-Wide Seder: GI Passover in World War II," *The Jewish Digest* 8 (1962).
4 Rabbi Joseph B. Soloveitchik, *Festival of Freedom: Essays on Pesah and the Haggadah,* edited by Joel B. Wolowelsky and Reuven Ziegler (Ktav, 2006), 40.
5 Ibid.
6 David Brooks, "The Orthodox Surge," *New York Times,* March 8, 2013, section A, 25.
7 George Weigel, "A Better Concept of Freedom," *First Things* (March 2002), 113.
8 Ibid.
9 Ibid.

10 Yuval Levin, "Taking the Long Way – Disciplines of the Soul Are the Basis of a Liberal Society," *First Things* (October 2014).
11 Marshall Weiss, "How DeMille Created a Sanctuary Out of the Exodus," *Forward*, December 5, 2003.

Israel Independence Day and Jerusalem Day

1 Margalit Fox, "Rabbi Who Cried to the Jews of Buchenwald: 'You Are Free,'" *New York Times*, March 27, 2013, section A, 1.
2 Milton Himmelfarb and Gertrude Himmelfarb, *Jews and Gentiles* (Encounter, 2007), 141.
3 https://www.commentary.org/articles/paul-johnson-3/the-miracle.
4 Ibid.
5 Rabbi Joseph B. Soloveitchik, *Kol Dodi Dofek*, translated by David Z. Gordon (Yeshiva University, 2006), 33.
6 J. R. R. Tolkien, *The Hobbit* (HarperCollins, 2012), 330.
7 "Iconic Six-Day War Photo Recreated at Western Wall," *Ynet Magazine*, December 17, 2014.
8 Yossi Klein Halevi, "The Photograph: A Search for June 1967," *Azure* 29 (Summer 2007).
9 Ibid.
10 Norman Podhoretz, "Jerusalem: The Scandal of Particularity," *Commentary* (July/August 2007).
11 Chaim Weizmann, *Trial and Error: The Autobiography of Chaim Weizmann* (Jewish Publication Society, 1949), 144.
12 Halevi, "The Photograph: A Search for June 1967."
13 Israel Meir Lau, Jessica Setbon, and Shira L. Schmidman, *Out of the Depths: The Story of a Child of Buchenwald Who Returned Home at Last – Chief Rabbi Israel Meir Lau*, translated from Hebrew by Jessica Setbon and Shira Leibowitz Schmidt (Sterling, 2005), 67–68.
14 Ibid.

Shavuot

1 *The Diary of Samuel Pepys*, entry for October 14, 1663, ed. Richard Le Gallienne (Modern Library Classics, 2003), 106.
2 C. S. Lewis, *Reflections on the Psalms*, 55.
3 Ibid.

4 Rabbi Joseph B. Soloveitchik, *Halakhic Man*, 40th Anniversary Edition, translated by Lawrence J. Kaplan (Jewish Publication Society, 2023), 37–38.
5 Ibid., 94–95.
6 R. R. Reno, "Loving the Law – Rabbi Joseph Soloveitchik Provides the Antidotes to Christianity's Antinomian Temptations," *First Things* (January 2012), 147–148.
7 Charles J. Chaput, "Yeshiva Lessons," *First Things* (August 2012), 148–149.
8 Ibid.
9 Yisrael Kashkin, "My Long Lonely Journey to the Rav," *Tradition* 45, no. 4 (2012): 56–57.
10 S. J. Dubner, *Turbulent Souls* (HarperCollins, 1999), 178–179.
11 Ibid.

Tishah BeAv

1 Stuart E. Eizenstat, *President Carter: The White House Years* (Thomas Dunne Books, 2018), 456.
2 Daniel Gordis, *Menachem Begin: The Battle for Israel's Soul* (Schocken, 2014), 35–36.
3 J. F. Schachter, "Case Study: Diagnosis and Treatment of a Psychotic Depressive," *The Torah U-Madda Journal* 9 (2000): 134–141.
4 Rabbi Joseph B. Soloveitchik, *Out of the Whirlwind: Essays on Mourning, Suffering and the Human Condition* (Ktav, 2003), 14.
5 Ibid., 17.
6 Michal Avera Samuel, "We Did Not Know: How Ethiopian Jews Discovered the Second Temple Was Gone," July 17, 2018, https:// blogs.timesofisrael.com/we-did-not-know-how-ethiopian-jews-discovered-the-second-temple-was-gone/.
7 Ibid.
8 William H. Seward, *William H. Seward's Travel Around the World* (D. Appleton and Company, 1876), 652–653.
9 Schachter, "Case Study," 141.
10 Yehuda Avner, *The Prime Ministers: An Intimate Narrative of Israeli Leadership* (Toby Press, 2010), 490–491.
11 Ibid.

Image Credits

Page xv, © NASA Archive / Alamy Stock Photo; page xvi, Courtesy of the Ramon Foundation; pages 1 and 9, © The Picture Art Collecn tion / Alamy Stock Photo; page 3, © KHM-Museumsverband; page 10, © Artefact / Alamy Stock Photo; page 12, © The State Hermitage Museum, St. Petersburg, photo by Vladmir Terebenin; page 14, Leo Baeck Institute; pages 17 and 20, © Tel Aviv Museum of Art; page 19, National Gallery Victoria; page 23, © National Maritime Museum, Greenwich, London; page 32, Rembrandt Harmensz van Rijn: Moses with the Tablets of the Law, 1659; Photo credits: Staatliche Museen zu Berlin, Gemäldegalerie / Christoph Schmidt; Public Domain Mark 1.0; pages 35 and 46, By Foto: Johann Werfring, CC BY-SA 3.0; page 42, Photo: © Shai Halevi , Courtesy of the Israel Antiqs uities Authority; page 43, Photo © The Israel Museum, Jerusalem; page 50, © David Blumenfeld; page 51, Photo by Marcos Schonr holz / Courtesy The Arava Institute ; pages 53 and 63 Photo © The Israel Museum Jerusalem by Elie Posner; page 55, © ImageBroker.com/Fabian von Poser; page 59, © Yael Yolovitch , Courtesy of the Israel Antiquities Authority; page 64, Steerpike (talk); page 65, © CNP Collection / Alamy Stock Photo; pages 69 and 80, © Naom Chen; page 73, © Hanan Isachar / Alamy Stock Photo; page 74, CC BY-SA 3.0 Chixoy (talk | contribs); page 79, Government Press Office, David Eldan, Public Domain; page 80, top © World History Archive / Alamy Stock Photo, bottom, © Noam Chen; pages 81 and

84, National Library of Israel, "Ktiv" Project.; page 85, The Metropolitan Museum of Art; page 92, Björtstraumur (talk | contribs); page 94, DcoetzeeBot (talk | contribs); page 95, © Shutterstock / photok sounds - Mindaugas Dulinskas; pages 99 and 115, Courtesy, L. Tom Perry Special Collections, Harold B. Lee Library, Brigham Young University. Cecil B. DeMille Archive; page 101, © Photo 12 / Alamy Stock Photo; page 109, © The British Library Board; MS Add. 27210, f. 15r; 110, Jonund (talk | contribs); page 115, Courtesy, L. Tom Perry Special Collections, Harold B. Lee Library, Brigham Young University. Cecil B. DeMille Archive; pages 117 and 127 Larry Koester CC BY 2.0; page 121, © Sam Churchill Photography; page 123, By Micha Perry / IDF Spokesperson's Unit; page 125, Government Press Office, Public Domain; page 128, Government Press Office, David Rubinger, Public Domain; page 131, by Meyer W. Weisgal (editor), Theodor Herzl: A Memorial, New York: The New Palestine, 1929, האתר להנצחת זכרה של גולדה מאיר, Public Domain, https://commons.wikimedia.org/w/index.php?curid=6370968; pages 135 and 137, by Solomon Hart – 4QGdmRAqxG-nRA at Google Cultural Institute maximum zoom level, Public Domain; page 138, © Universal Art Archive / Alamy Stock Photo; page 139, © public domain; page 141 Photo by Arthur P. Strong © Ingrid Franzon;Photo; 145, The Jewish Museum NY Public Domain; pages 151 and 162, by Gustav Bauernfeind (1848–1904), Public Domain; page 156, Government Press Office, Ya'acov Sa'ar, Public Domain ; page 160, Government Press Office, Moshe Milner, Public Domain; pages 162 & 165, by Gustav Bauernfeind (1848–1904), Public Domain; page 169, Government Press Office, Moshe Milner, Public Domain.

The fonts used in this book are from the Arno family

Maggid Books
The best of contemporary Jewish thought from
Koren Publishers Jerusalem